G000122998

Inter...

...siness English

English for
BUSINESS LIFE

IAN BADGER PETE MENZIES

Course Book

with detachable Business
Grammar Guide
and Answer Key

HEINLE
CENGAGE Learning™

Australia • Brazil • Japan • Korea • Mexico • Singapore • Spain • United Kingdom • United States

HEINLE
CENGAGE Learning

English for Business Life Intermediate Coursebook
Ian Badger and Pete Menzies

Publisher: Nick Sheard

Head of Inventory: Jane Glendening

Head of Production and Manufacturing: Alissa McWhinnie

Production Controller: Tom Relf

© 2006 Heinle, Cengage Learning

ALL RIGHTS RESERVED. No part of this work covered by the copyright herein may be reproduced, transmitted, stored or used in any form or by any means graphic, electronic, or mechanical, including but not limited to photocopying, recording, scanning, digitizing, taping, Web distribution, information networks, or information storage and retrieval systems, except as permitted under Section 107 or 108 of the 1976 United States Copyright Act, or applicable copyright law of another jurisdiction, without the prior written permission of the publisher.

For permission to use material from this text or product, submit all requests online at **cengage.com/permissions.**

Further permissions questions can be emailed to **permissionrequest@cengage.com.**

ISBN: 978-0-462-00763-2

Heinle, Cengage Learning EMEA
Cheriton House, North Way, Andover, Hampshire, SP10 5BE, United Kingdom

Cengage Learning is a leading provider of customised learning solutions with office locations around the globe, including Singapore, the United Kingdom, Australia, Mexico, Brazil and Japan. Locate our local office at: **international.cengage.com/region**

Cengage Learning products are represented in Canada by Nelson Education Ltd.

Visit Heinle online at **elt.heinle.com**
Visit our corporate website at **cengage.com**

Acknowledgements
The authors would like to thank the following for their advice and support in the preparation of English for Business Life: Simon Ross, Lucy Brodie, Christie Catalano, Keith Dalton, Jo Barker, Graham Hart, Teresa Miller and Fiona Walker. Our special thanks go to Valerie Lambert for her work on the Business Grammar Guide. We would also like to thank our business 'students' from organisations including UPM-Kymmene Oyj, Metso Paper, BEMIS, Vattenfall, the International Maritime Organisation, GE Finance, ABN Amro (Investment Bank), Dresdner Kleinwort Wasserstein (UK), Panasonic Europe, Nokia and Marketing Akademie Hamburg for providing the inspiration and feedback that underpins English for Business Life. Finally, the authors would like to thank their families for their support and forbearance during the writing process! – Gerry, Ollie and Elly Badger, Helen Glavin and Miranda Glavin.

Photo Acknowledgements
Pg 13 C. Devan/Zefa/Corbis, Pg 14 (L) Grace/Zefa/Corbis, (R) H. Stilton/Zefa/Corbis, Pg 15 Ryan McVay /Getty, Pg 17 Ariel Skelley/Corbis, Pg 19 Romilly Lockyer/Getty, Pg 20 Felix Clouzot/Getty, Pg 21 OnRequest, Inc./Alamy, Pg 22 C. Devan/Zefa/Corbis, Pg 2531 Yellow Dog Productions/Corbis, Pg 27 A Room With Views/Alamy, Pg 29 Still Pictures, Pg 30 Still Pictures, Pg 31 vattenfall.com, Pg 33 Sebastien Starr/Gettty, Pg 34 lonelyplanetimages.com, Pg 37 David Sacks/Getty. Pg 39 Jochem Wijnands/Alamy, Pg 41 Arcaid, Pg 43 Henry Arden/Zefa/Corbis, Pg 45 Norman Jung/Zeta/ Corbis, Pg 46 (L) Emely/Zeta/Corbis, (R) Chabruken/Getty, Pg 47 Courtesy w3.org, Pg 49 Taxi/Getty, Pg 53/56 Courtesy Cameron Balloons, Pg 57 David Olver/Getty Pg 59 Blickwinkel/Alamy, Pg 61 lonelyplanetimages.com, Pg 63 safrdig.com, Pg 65 JLP/Sylvia Torres/Corbis, Pg 66 Helen King/Corbis, Pg 69 Arcaid, Pg 70 Rex Features, Pg 71 Steven Puetzer/Getty, Pg 73 Taxi/Getty, Pg 74 Setboun/Corbis, Pg 75 Alex Mares-Manton/Getty, Pg 77 Rex Features, Pg 79 Marc Romanelli/Getty, Pg 81 dubairacingclub.com, Pg 82 Rex Features, Pg 85 Corbis, Pg 86 Ed Holub/Photex/Zefa/Corbis, Pg 89 VCL/Chris Ryan/Getty, Pg 91 Helen King/Corbis, Pg 93 Ronnie Kaufman/Corbis, Pg 94 Rex Features, Pg 95 Lucia Zeccara/Corbis, Pg 97 lonelyplanetimages.com, Pg 98 4cornersimages.com, Pg 101 Gregory Bajor/Alamy, Pg 102 Jon Feingersh/Zefa/Corbis, Pg 105 Larry Dale Gordon/Zefa/Corbis, Pg 106 Tibor Bognar/Corbis, Pg 107 4cornersimages.com, Pg 109 R. Holz/Zefa/Corbis, Pg 111 Felix Clouzot/Getty, Pg 113 Falko Updarp/Zefa/Corbis, Pg114 Gary Buss/Getty, Pg 117 John Francis Bourke/Getty, Pg 118 LWA-Dann Tardif/Zefa/Corbis, Pg 121 G Baden/Zefa/Corbis, Pg 122 Steven Peters/Getty, Pg 123 Peter Cade/Getty, Pg 125 Getty, Pg 130 Dennis Cooper/Zefa/Corbis

Printed in China by RR Donnelley
4 5 6 7 8 9 10 – 13 12 11

Contents

Contents chart

UNIT	EXPRESSIONS	LANGUAGE FOCUS	PRACTICE
1 Everyday business contacts	I use English every day in my work. Are you busy? I'm calling about Thursday's meeting. Can I call you back this afternoon? We open at 8am, Eastern Standard Time.	Articles (*a/an* and *the*) *some* and *any* Time differences (*They're on GMT.*) Seasons and festivals (*It's a public holiday.*)	Discussing language needs Beginning and ending telephone calls Voicemail messages Passing on messages
2 Developing contacts	Have you got any contacts in Central America? I know several people in the tourism business. Let me give you some names and addresses. We met last week. I'm a friend of Rakesh Singh's.	*much, many* and *a lot (of)* *(a) few, several, (a) little* *so* and *such (a)* Time references (*next month, the week before last,* etc.) Personal qualities	Exploring contacts Multinational terms A letter of introduction
3 Out of the office	I'm trying to contact Tony Lopez. Do you know how I can get in touch with him? I'll give you his mobile number. Shall I get him to call you in the morning?	Making requests (*Could/Would you …?, Would you mind …?*) Making offers (*Shall/Can I …? Would you like me to …?*) Mobile phone language	Making contact outside working hours Arranging to meet and socialising Leaving messages Contacting someone urgently
4 Introducing your company	We're a public limited company. Our annual turnover is approximately £2.5m. Tommy Hoe is the chief accountant. Our head office is just outside Paris.	Prepositions of place (*at, near, outside,* etc.) Phrases of location (*not far from, to the left of,* etc.) High numbers (*two point five billion*)	Providing background information about a company Describing location and layout
5 Company profiles	It's a state-owned power company. I believe it's run like a private company. Basically, we make and distribute electricity. We're the region's largest producer of gas.	*make* and *do* (*make an effort, do worse,* etc.) Present Simple vs. the Present Continuous Verbs normally used in the simple form (*think, want,* etc.)	Giving a brief description of a company Profiling a public utility company

UNIT	EXPRESSIONS	LANGUAGE FOCUS	PRACTICE
6 Competitors	What's the competition like in North Africa? We're more profitable than our competitors. Their prices are less competitive. They can't (cannot) compete on price.	Comparative and superlative adjectives (*far greater, the best*, etc.) *less/least* in comparisons Expressing opinions (*I don't think/believe ...*, etc.) Geographical areas (*Eastern Europe, Central America*, etc.)	Comparing companies How to beat the competition
7 Your personal background	I was born in Spain. I'm self-employed. How long have you lived in Algiers? What do you do in your free time? I spend most of my time gardening.	The Present Perfect tense *have to* and *have/had to* *still* *yet*	Giving personal background information Giving personal news
8 Conditions of work	What's your office like to work in? What kind of benefits do you get? Where were you working this time last year? I tried to contact you, but you had already gone home.	Past Continuous tense Past Perfect tense *too/enough* (e.g. *too heavy to lift, not enough space for us all*) Some office equipment/furniture	Features of a good office environment Talking about perks and benefits Talking about salary packages
9 Job descriptions	He's responsible for running ... She doesn't have much to do with the finance side. What's she like? She's very hard-working. She's quite tall with straight, dark hair.	Replying to negative sentences Describing appearance and dress Adjectives and their opposites (*safe/unsafe*, etc.) Recommending and suggesting (*Have you thought of ...?, I think you should ...*, etc.)	Describing your previous jobs Talking about the job you do Making suggestions and recommendations A brief job history
10 Buying products	Our products are extremely well made. The reference number is 12/473-AZ9. Do you still stock it? We used to supply it in green. We don't make it in that size any more.	*used to* (*You used to supply ...*) Adverbs in phrases (*highly competitive*, etc.) Numbers and symbols Materials and substances (*steel, concrete*, etc.)	Ordering products Key selling points Making a product enquiry

UNIT	EXPRESSIONS	LANGUAGE FOCUS	PRACTICE
11 Product descriptions	We have been selling this line for 20 years. They range in size from 3 metres to 4³/₄ metres. They are made in a range of shapes and colours. I'd like a round one. Do you know if they are still available?	Present Perfect Continuous tense Present Simple Passive tense Indirect questions (*Do you know whether …?*) Shapes (*square, rectangular*, etc.)	Checking product information Promotional gifts Describing your product
12 Faults and breakdowns	There's something wrong with it. It needs sorting out. I'll contact the person whose job it is to mend it. I'll speak to the person who dealt with it. We're very pleased with the new Korean model.	Relative pronouns (*which, whose*, etc.) The order of adjectives *need + -ing* (*It needs mending*)	Expressing satisfaction and dissatisfaction with a product Discussing a faulty product
13 The services you provide and use	Some work is done by an outside contractor. We do the other work ourselves. We must get this machine serviced. What would it cost to lease it?	*to have/get something done ought to* Reflexive pronouns (*myself*, etc.) *own* (*We handle our own cleaning.*) Payment times (*per week*, etc.)	Discussing reasons for using services Discussing a range of services Considering whether to lease or purchase
14 Service issues	We regret that we have had to cancel the course. We've just heard that the delivery hasn't arrived. It should have arrived by now. We apologise for any inconvenience. You should have let us know sooner.	Past tense of modal verbs (*You should have/could have ought to …*) Apologising Accepting and rejecting apologies	Making and dealing with complaints Sorting out a delivery problem Customer service
15 Service industries	According to ABL, the deal is worth $300 million. They can't (cannot) have said that. I must have misunderstood. How much does the contract include? How much do they charge?	Correcting misunderstandings Fees and charges (*What do you charge for …?*) Jobs in service industries *like/such as*	Researching a catering service Identifying service industries Reasons for choosing a supplier

UNIT	EXPRESSIONS	LANGUAGE FOCUS	PRACTICE
16 Looking after visitors	I was thinking of getting tickets to the opera. Would you rather go out to dinner? What should I wear? Should I take a gift? We mustn't be late.	*prefer* and *would rather* *mustn't, needn't* and *don't have to* *was/were going/planning to* Giving advice (*You should always* …, etc.)	Planning an evening out Deciding where to go Cultural sensitivities
17 Hotels and restaurants	We booked a table for eight o'clock. Excuse me, we're ready to order. I'd like the salmon. They told me the fish was excellent. How much should I add for service?	Reported speech (*He said he would the following day*) *say* vs. *tell* *speak* vs. *talk* Hotel and restaurant vocabulary	Entertaining guests in a hotel Ordering a meal
18 Corporate entertaining	The event begins at 10am and lasts four hours. I'd like the standard package. The reception went very well. It went better than last year. Both teams played really well.	Spelling and position of adverbs Comparative adverbs Some sports vocabulary (*Good shot!*)	Arranging hospitality for customers Tailoring a hospitality package
19 Setting up meetings	I thought I'd (I had) better call you. Are you still OK for the 27th? We're meeting to talk about the new contract. It looks as if Friday is going to be difficult. Would you be able to meet on Thursday?	*had better* *be able to* *look as if/though* and *sounds as if/though* Punctuation marks	Arranging a time and place to meet Rearranging meetings Agendas
20 Meeting procedures	There are four main topics on the agenda. Let's start with item 1. As you know, I'm in favour of the plan. In the first paragraph, it says … If I were you, I'd (I would) check the facts.	Phrases used in meetings Second Conditional Expressing agreement and disagreement Referring to documents (*If you look at line 4* …)	Preparing an agenda Meeting targets A meeting to discuss a ban on smoking

UNIT	EXPRESSIONS	LANGUAGE FOCUS	PRACTICE
21 Meeting follow-up	Did you manage to cover all the points? Are you going to circulate the minutes? Did you remember to send a copy to …? Freda asked me to send a draft to Hella. We arranged to meet again on the 11th.	More reported speech Verbs followed by the infinitive	Organising a successful meeting Checking action steps Follow-up to a meeting A follow-up phone call
22 Arranging a visit	I'm calling on behalf of Dr Salem. He'll be staying in Boston for six days. He'd like to visit you during his stay. Will you be coming by taxi? Tell the cab driver to follow the signs to Bridgeport.	Future tenses The Future Continuous tense (*I'll be working in Boston* …) *while, during* and *for*	Checking an itinerary Preparing for a visit Giving directions from an airport
23 Abroad on business	I find it difficult to sleep on planes. I won't sleep till I get to Berlin. Where are you staying while you're in Germany? Can I have a return ticket to Amsterdam, please?	*when, as soon as, while, before*, etc. in future sentences Some travel vocabulary *easy/difficult to*, etc.	Advice on jet lag Some travel situations Transport delays
24 Returning from a business trip	I'm just back from a trip to … It's the third most important state in the region. How far is it from the capital? It's about eight kilometres south-east of … I'd better write my report today, in case they need it tomorrow.	*How far …?* and *a long way How long …?* and *a long time in case* (*in case it rains*) Points of the compass Rankings (*second largest*, etc.)	Reporting back on a trip Commenting on accommodation
25 Personal finances	About 24% of my income goes in tax. We pay our regular outgoings by direct debit. My financial situation is very different from yours. I spend about half as much as you do on …	*do* and *did* for emphasis Some financial vocabulary Some insurance terms Fractions and multiples (*half/twice as much as* …)	Personal expenses Turnover and expenses

UNIT	EXPRESSIONS	LANGUAGE FOCUS	PRACTICE
26 Company finances	The company announced its results in November. Net assets are in the region of £40 million. What was your turnover last year? We have set tough targets for the coming year. The accounts were approved at the AGM.	Revision of the Passive tense Some common business abbreviations (*a/c, AGM, b/f,* etc.)	Balance sheet terms An annual review of a company Comparing company performance
27 Payment issues	I'm calling about our invoice. It was for 25 manuals at $25 each. According to our records, it was paid two weeks ago. Apparently, there was a problem with it. We will take no action providing we receive payment within 14 days.	*unless* and *provided/providing apparently it seems that* Prepositions related to payment Numbers and calculations	Requesting payment Invoice details Explaining non-payment of an invoice
28 Preparing for a presentation	I'm calling to check what equipment you need. I'll need a projector. I look forward to meeting you next week. She's very good at handling questions. I'm used to working in all kinds of situations.	Verb + preposition + *-ing* (*I apologise for being late.*) Likes and dislikes *to be used to* and *to get used to*	Improving presentation skills Checking equipment Making final preparations
29 Presenting facts and figures	The graph shows the total number of unemployed. The overall rate was just under 9%. The figure has gone down dramatically. The figures in the left-hand column represent average sales per branch. Only one in three of our sales is through supermarkets.	Numerical information Verb + infinitive or *-ing average* (*to average, on average,* etc.)	Describing a graph Historical trends Locating information Updating information
30 Delivering a presentation	First of all, I'll give you an overview. This table shows projected sales for the coming year. That brings me to my next point. Are there any questions? Even though it was short, it was very useful.	*because, as* and *since so* and *therefore although, even though, in spite of* Phrases used in presentations	Discussing presentations 'dos' and 'don'ts' Giving a presentation Presenting information

Introduction

English for Business Life is a four-level course designed for people who need English for their everyday work.

English for Business Life is:

- a course written by authors with a wide experience of teaching English for business in a range of international contexts, countries and cultures
- a course that respects the modern need for flexibility; learners can follow fast, standard or comprehensive tracks through the materials
- a course that follows a progressive and comprehensive grammar syllabus, with the stress on the effective use of grammar for clear communication
- a course that satisfies the requirements of the Common European Framework, BEC and equivalent global testing authorities
- a course that supports the learner in a highly connected modern world.

The Intermediate level of the course consists of:

- a course book with detachable answer key and grammar reference booklet
- course book listening exercises on CD
- a self-study guide packaged with an accompanying audio CD
- a trainer's manual.

Learners can follow fast, standard and comprehensive tracks through the material – 45 to 90 hours of work:

- fast track – 45 hours
- standard track – 60 hours
- comprehensive track – 90 hours.

Summary of components

Course Book

The Course Book consists of:

- 30 units
- support materials where necessary
- a glossary of business-related terms
- a grammar/language index
- audioscripts of all listening activities
- business grammar guide and answer key in separate booklets.

Two audio CDs are available as a separate component.

Self-study guide

The Self-study guide consists of:

- 30 parallel units
- material that can be used in support of the course book or as a self-standing resource
- audio CD containing recordings of core language, pronunciation points and listening exercises
- reinforcement/consolidation exercises
- a grammar/language reference section
- a glossary of business-related terms.

Trainer's manual

The trainer's manual consists of:

- notes on exercises and ideas for consolidation/extension work
- a glossary of business-related terms
- notes on business practice
- answers and audioscripts for Course Book exercises
- progress tests.

Business English exams/testing equivalence

Levels	Common European Framework Level	ALTE	BEC	London Chamber of Commerce (EFB)
Upper Intermediate	C1–C2	4	Higher	Level 3
Intermediate	B2–C1	3	Vantage	Level 2
Pre-intermediate	B1–B2	2	Preliminary	Level 1
Elementary	A2–B1			Preliminary/ Level 1

Useful websites

For more on the European Framework visit www.alte.org
For BEC visit www.cambridgeesol.org/exams/bec.htm
For the Business Language Testing Service visit www.bulats.org
For the London Chamber of Commerce Exams visit www.lccieb.com
For the TOEIC American exams for working people visit www.ets.org/, then click on TOEIC

A range of training situations

English for Business Life presents the language that is essential for doing business in English; it has strong global relevance. Groups that will benefit from using the materials include:

- business schools and colleges
- language schools which offer English for business courses
- company training courses and study programmes
- vocational adult education classes
- schools and colleges which aim to equip their students with the language skills they will need in their working lives.

The intermediate level

The Intermediate level of **English for Business Life** is for you if you have studied English for perhaps three to six years at school and/or college. You will probably be able to use the language with a fair degree of fluency. However, although you will be able to 'get by' in most situations requiring English, your level of fluency and accuracy may not be as high as the level demanded in your current or future work.

This course will help you to improve your ability to use English in a wide range of business and business-related social situations. It will also be of interest if you have a higher level of general English, but need, specifically, to improve your English for business communication.

Content

The materials cover everyday business speaking, listening, reading and writing skills, through a range of guided and free exercises. The aim is to find out what you can do in English within a given theme and then to help you to develop your skills.

Each unit contains one listening exercise (overview) which encapsulates the target language of the unit and others which develop sensitivity to different types of English, in line with the fact that English is very often used as an international language of communication between speakers of many nationalities.

Each unit also contains a number of study points – grammar and vocabulary. The language focus sections are concerned specifically with helping you to use the language accurately for effective and clear communication. The book also contains a glossary of business-related language plus there is a business grammar guide in a separate booklet.

There are additional language notes, exercises and a copy of the business grammar guide in the Self-study guide.

Flexibility: different tracks through the materials

Fast track: 45 hours (approximately 1.5 hours per unit) involving, for example:

- introductory discussion on each theme
- language focus
- listening – overview
- practice activities.

Standard track: 60 hours (approximately 2 hours per unit) involving, for example:

- introductory discussion on each theme
- practice activities
- language focus
- listening – overview
- application exercises
- study notes and selected exercises from the Self-study guide.

Comprehensive track: 90 hours (approximately 3 hours per unit) involving, for example:

- introductory discussion on each theme
- reading/practice activities
- language focus
- listening – overview + additional listening exercises
- application exercises
- detailed study of related Self-study guide materials.

Some study tips

- Make time for your English studies. Approach them with the same level of commitment that you would any other project in your work or spare time.
- Find the study pattern that works best for you. In our view 'little and often' is more effective than occasional long sessions.
- Keep an organised study file. Make sure that the language that is most relevant to your needs is clearly highlighted.
- Ensure that you relate the language presented in the course back to your area of business or study. If there are terms you need which are not included in the material, consult your trainer, English-speaking colleagues and friends, and make thorough notes.
- Make use of the English-speaking media – web pages, radio, TV, professional journals, magazines and newspapers to follow up your business and leisure interests in English.
- Make use of monolingual and bilingual dictionaries. A number of dictionaries are available on-line and the 'synonym' and 'thesaurus' keys on your computer are always useful.
- Use the Self-study guide which accompanies this Couse Book (30–45 hours of study).

Study themes in *English for Business Life*

Intermediate level

- Contacts
- Companies
- Personnel
- Products and services
- Entertaining
- Meetings
- Travel
- Money and finance
- Presentations

Other levels

Elementary level

- You and your job
- Your company
- Brief exchanges
- Arrangements
- Telephoning
- Business hospitality
- Business trips
- Your working environment
- Enquiring and booking

Pre-intermediate level

- You and your company
- Meeting people
- Time off
- The workplace
- Numbers and figures
- Business travel
- The product
- Arrangements
- Business entertaining
- Sales and selling
- Requesting/supplying information

Upper intermediate level

- Business travel
- Following up
- Dealing with change
- Culture and values
- Conferences and exhibitions
- Networking
- Delivering quality
- Work/life balance
- Feedback and review

The authors

IAN BADGER has extensive experience of developing courses and systems of language training for business, and is a regular speaker at international conferences. He is a partner in Business and Medical English Services, and a director of English4 Ltd (www.english4.com). He is series editor of *English for Work*, and his publications include *Everyday Business English*, *Everyday Business Writing* and *Business English Phrases*.

PETE MENZIES is an associate of Pod (Professional and Organisational Development) and founder of Commnet, a dedicated training agency specialising in written communication and email management. Awards for his published work include the Duke of Edinburgh ESU Prize and the Gold Medal at the Leipzig Industrial Fair.

UNIT 1 Everyday business contacts

1 | Overview

Key dialogues

1 Listen to the dialogues and answer the questions.

   a What does Mary Patel want?
   Where is Paul Smyk's boss?

   b Why is the office closed?
   What message does Sam leave?

   c Who is Manuel Farkas?
   What time is it in Mexico?

   d How good is his English in face-to-face situations?
   How good is his written English?

Preparation

Prepare for this unit by thinking about when you need to use English. How do you usually communicate in English? By email, by phone, in face-to-face situations?

How have your needs changed over the years? Can you identify any problems which you have when communicating with colleagues and customers in different countries?

Refer to the Language Notes and Useful Phrases in the Language Reference section on page 16.

2 | Practice

When do you need English?

1 Work in pairs. Find out about your partner's language needs.

Questionnaire

How often do you use English …
… with colleagues?
… with customers/clients?
… with superiors/bosses?
… with employees who report to you?
… with friends?
… other?

How often do you use English to …
… make arrangements?
… welcome visitors?
… talk on the phone?
… write emails, formal letters, faxes, etc?
… write instant messages, send text messages?
… other?

How often do you have communication problems because of …
… time differences?
… different working hours?
… local accents?
… cultural differences?
… other?

every day	twice a week	once a week	every now and then

2 As a group, discuss the findings. Give specific examples of communication problems and how you have tried to overcome them.

3 Language focus

Articles: and some/any

1 Refer to the Language Notes on page 16 and complete the sentences with *a*, *the*, *some*, *any* or –. In some cases, there is more than one possibility.

   a Have you got .... today's newspaper?
   b Have you seen .... paper?
   c I bought .... interesting magazine today.
   d We need .... new equipment.
   e Have you heard .... latest news?
   f We don't have .... problems with .... new machine.
   g My assistant never does .... work.
   h .... standard of his work is very poor.
   i I have .... information for you.
   j I've got .... new job.

Seasons and festivals

2 Work in pairs. Discuss which of these festivals you celebrate and which your overseas contacts celebrate. Are there any other festivals which you celebrate which are not listed below?

When do they occur?
How do you celebrate them?
How do you greet someone on that day?
Do they cause any inconvenience?

▶ Ramadan	▶ Chinese New Year
▶ Christmas	▶ Passover
▶ May Day	▶ Boxing Day
▶ Thanksgiving	▶ Easter
▶ Independence Day	▶ Divali

Time differences

3 Notice these ways of talking about time differences.

   – We open at 8am; that's four in the afternoon Korean time. We're eight hours behind you.
   – They arrive at eleven o'clock Eastern Standard Time. That's 2pm your time. You are three hours ahead.
   – Sorry, I didn't mean to wake you up. I forgot you were in Shanghai. I thought you were still in Berlin.

In pairs, practise talking about time differences. Make calls to these cities.

a Seoul   **b** Istanbul   **c** Moscow   **d** Colombo   **e** Shanghai

4 | Application

Beginning and ending telephone calls

Practise short phone conversations in pairs. Use the table as necessary.

Beginning a call

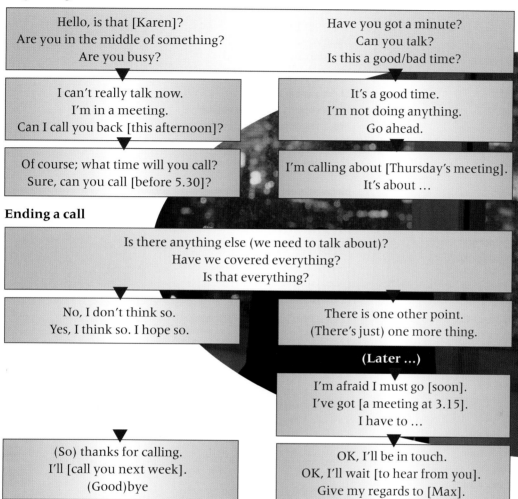

Hello, is that [Karen]? Are you in the middle of something? Are you busy?	Have you got a minute? Can you talk? Is this a good/bad time?

▼

I can't really talk now. I'm in a meeting. Can I call you back [this afternoon]?	It's a good time. I'm not doing anything. Go ahead.

Of course; what time will you call? Sure, can you call [before 5.30]?	I'm calling about [Thursday's meeting]. It's about …

Ending a call

Is there anything else (we need to talk about)? Have we covered everything? Is that everything?

▼

No, I don't think so. Yes, I think so. I hope so.	There is one other point. (There's just) one more thing.

(Later …)

I'm afraid I must go [soon]. I've got [a meeting at 3.15]. I have to …

(So) thanks for calling. I'll [call you next week]. (Good)bye	OK, I'll be in touch. OK, I'll wait [to hear from you]. Give my regards to [Max].

5 | Listening

Telephone conversations

1 Listen to the four conversations and indicate in which conversation the points are mentioned. (a, b, etc.)

not in yet ☐	in the building somewhere ☐
at lunch ☐	has a new number ☐
ill or on sick leave ☐	away this week ☑ a
on holiday ☐	in a meeting ☐
with some visitors ☐	away from his/her desk ☐

2 Write a short message or email for the people concerned. Note the message for Milan which relates to conversation **a**.

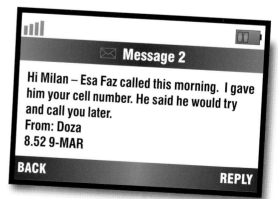

Message 2

Hi Milan – Esa Faz called this morning. I gave him your cell number. He said he would try and call you later.
From: Doza
8.52 9-MAR

BACK   REPLY

LANGUAGE REFERENCE

Language notes

For more detailed notes, see the Business Grammar Guide.

Some uses of *a/an*

Note the following examples of *a/an*.

e.g. A man called for you earlier.
    Matt was an excellent boss.
    It's a European project.
    I've had an interesting idea.
    Can I take a message?
    I'd like a cup of coffee.

Note that if a noun is uncountable or plural, we use *some/any* in place of *a/an*.

e.g. I brought some petrol.
    We need some information.
    Have you got any change?
    She is reading some reports.
    Are there any messages for me?

Some uses of *the*

Note the following examples of *the*.

e.g. I read the report you sent me.
    The government supports the plan.
    The people from CIT have arrived.
    It's the biggest company in the world.
    I'll meet you at the airport.
    Could you tell me the time, please?

Note when *the* is not used.

e.g. Money is very tight right now.
    We make shoes for children.
    It's Independence Day.
    I haven't got time to talk now.
    I had lunch with Tom.
    I came by car.

Note when *the* is used in names.

e.g. I work for Goldwell.
    I work for the Goldwell company.
    Fazer is head of Finance.
    He runs the finance department.
    He lives in America.
    He lives in the USA.
    I have booked a room at the Hilton .
    Do you have a copy of the *Times*?

Some uses of *some* and *any*

Affirmative:
We need some samples.
We need some stationery.
You could order some.

Negative:
They can't give us any information.
They don't have any leaflets.
We don't need any.

Interrogative:
Have you got some/any biscuits/milk?
Did you ask for some/any?
Where can I get some?

Short answers:
Have you got any spare copies?
Yes, I've got some. No, I haven't got any.
Yes, some.   No, none.

(Note that we do not use the short answer *No, not any.*)

Useful phrases

Hello, is that Mrs Friedman?
Speaking.   It's Jan here.
Are you busy?   Is this a good time to talk?
Can you talk?
Yes, go ahead.

Is it about Thursday?
I'm sorry, I'm in a meeting.
Can I call you back this afternoon?

Could I speak to the sales manager?
Is Harry Pontia there?
He's on another line.
I'm afraid he isn't available.

We open at 8am Eastern Standard Time.
That's eleven o'clock your time.
You're three hours ahead of us.
It's a public holiday today.
There's no one in the office.

Can I take a message?
Can you give Maria a message?
Could you tell her that Rosa called?
Could you ask her to call me?

Do you have any time this afternoon?
No, but I have some free time tomorrow.
So, have we covered everything?
Is there anything else?
I think that's everything.   Thanks for calling.

How often do you use English in your job?
I use English every day.
I sometimes have problems on the phone.
The company's official language is English.

UNIT 2 Developing contacts

1 Overview

Key dialogues

Listen to the exchanges and answer the questions.

a Does the man have any contacts in Poland?
What does he offer to do?

b When and where did they meet?
Which company's contact details does he give?

c Why is the first speaker looking for a new accountant?
Why does the second speaker recommend her accountant?

d Why does Mary Page contact Rakesh Singh?
How does he help her?

Preparation

Bring to class your contact list/address book. These materials will be useful as you go through the unit.

Prepare for the lesson by thinking about how you develop your networks of business contacts – for example, at trade fairs, conferences and chambers of commerce.

Refer to the Useful Phrases and Language Notes for this unit, which are on page 20.

2 Practice

Exploring contacts

1 Find out about the people your fellow learners know. Work in pairs, using the language boxes as a guide.

a Contacts in different geographical locations

> Who do you know in [Lodz]?
> Have you got any contacts in [Poland]?
> Do you know anyone in [Atlanta]?
> I've got a few contacts in [Milan].

b Contacts in different professions/occupations

> Do you know a good [lawyer]?
> What is your [accountant] like?
> Do you have a good [tax adviser]?
> Who is the best [tour operator] in town?
> I can recommend [the people] we use.
> He/She is good to work with.

c Contacts in different businesses and industries

> Do you know anyone who sells [projectors]?
> ... who can supply .... ?
> ... who deals in .... ?
> ... who works in a [bank]?
> ... who works in [the construction business]?
> I know a very good [consultant].

2 Report back to the group on the contacts you have made.

e.g. Helen told me about a good designer in Budapest …
I asked Paulo to recommend some tour operators in Pisa. He gave me several names, including …

3 | Language focus

Refer to the Language Notes on page 20 as you do these exercises.

much, many *and* a lot (of)

1 Complete these sentences using *much, many* and *a lot (of)*. In some cases, there will be more than one possibility.

a I have got quite .... friends in Germany.

b I haven't got very .... to do tomorrow.

c There are .... things to arrange.

d Are there .... more calls to make? Yes, quite ....

e There isn't very .... enthusiasm for the project.

f There aren't .... days till the deadline.

g Have you got .... more work to do? No, not ....

several, (a) few *and* (a) little

2 Use *several, (a) few* and *(a) little* to complete these sentences so that they are true.

e.g. I know several *people who could help you.*

a We have very little ....

b There are quite a few ....

c We receive very few ....

d Would you like a little .... ?

e There are several ....

f There were a few ....

g We have quite a few ....

so *and* such (a)

3 Complete the sentences using *so* and *such (a)*.

a They have .... good contacts that …

b Everyone was .... helpful that …

c It would be difficult to find .... comfortable hotel in my country.

d There are .... many people I need to see.

e Why was the customer .... angry?

f We gave him .... good deal that …

g How did you get .... cheap deal?

h I have had .... much work to do recently.

4 | Talking point

Multinational teams

Read the article, using a dictionary where necessary. Then discuss in pairs the questions that follow.

Cultural differences present much greater problems than language for companies setting up multi-national teams or expanding into foreign countries, says a report published in *Personnel Management*.

Experts looked at problems in a British Petroleum office in Brussels combining 40 staff from 13 countries.

They found that while British members of the team consider working late to be a sign of loyalty and enthusiasm, Scandinavians think that it shows inefficiency or incompetence.

Another potential area for misunderstanding is rank. French executives believe authority comes with the job and do not expect their judgement to be challenged.

But managers from Britain, Scandinavia and the Netherlands want to have their decisions questioned, or at least discussed.

The authors found that the differences confirmed common stereotypes. Dutch managers wanted to discuss more and were more relaxed about management style. They were happy for subordinates to go above them for help.

The Germans, on the other hand, were anxious that decisions were put into operation quickly. They insisted on a more hierarchical management structure and, when invited to seek advice from more senior managers, thought that they were being 'set up'.

At the other end of the scale, Americans were astonished to find French colleagues wanting to shake hands every morning. They thought it excessively formal for day-to-day greetings. But the French considered it 'simple friendliness'.

From The Daily Telegraph

a What picture does the article give of British and French managers? Do you agree with this picture?

b What cultural differences have you noticed when dealing with other nationalities – on the telephone, for example?

c How do other nationalities stereotype your nationality?

d What is the stereotype view of the countries you deal with? Do these stereotypes have any basis in reality?

5 Listening

Time references

1 Listen to people following up a new contact. Match the time of the first meeting with the time of the next one.

   a last Tuesday   **i** next month
   b a couple of days ago   **ii** the month after next
   c the week before last   **iii** a week on Monday

2 Refer to the Language Notes on time references (page 20). In pairs, arrange to meet. Give alternative times.

   e.g. – I'm free on the 4th July or the 5th.
        – Isn't the 4th Independence Day?
        – You're right. Let's make it the 5th.

6 Application

A letter of introduction

1 Read the letter. Then fill in the gaps, using the terms in the box. Think about the information you would include in a letter of introduction.

How do you feel about making 'personal' comments in such letters. Are there any data protection issues in your country which prevent you from making such comments.

▸ branches	▸ colleague	▸ confident
▸ next month	▸ personality	▸ relationships
▸ responsible for	▸ to lose	

Santoro Consumer Electronis Srl

Via Fa di Bruno 37
016739 Roma
Tel: 0093-739-21049   Fax: 0092-739-076037

Wednesday 24th February
Ref: RS.PV1

Dear Benjamin

I am writing to introduce my **a** .... Ms Magda Grega, who will be joining your data processing systems planning department **b** .... As you probably know, she has been **c** .... office automation within the whole group, and we will be sorry **d** .... her. She has had an important role in coordinating dealings between the hardware and software suppliers and the company **e** .... , and has established excellent **f** .... throughout the company.

On a personal note, she is a likeable and energetic person with an outgoing **g** .... , who can be tough when necessary. I am **h** .... that you will enjoy working with her.

With best wishes

Rakesh Singh

Rakesh Singh
Deputy IT Director (Europe)

2 Check that you know these adjectives. Then write a letter or email introducing a colleague and referring to his/her personal qualities. Use the letter above as a guide.

▸ cheerful	▸ clever	▸ competent
▸ efficient	▸ energetic	▸ experienced
▸ friendly	▸ hard-working	▸ helpful
▸ highly qualified	▸ intelligent	▸ likeable
▸ outgoing	▸ quiet	▸ reliable
▸ self-confident	▸ tough	▸ warm

LANGUAGE REFERENCE

Language notes

For more detailed notes, see the Business Grammar Guide.

Some uses of *much*, *many*, *a lot (of)* and *lots (of)*

Affirmative:

There is (quite) a lot of interest in it.
There are (quite) a lot of messages for you.
Many companies are closing down.
There is lots (of work) to do.

Negative:

There isn't (very) much profit in it.
There isn't a lot of profit in it.
We haven't got (very) many competitors.
We haven't got a lot of competitors.
They don't sell much in Turkey.
They don't sell a lot there.

Interrogative:

How much money do you need?
How many pieces would you like?
Have you got much work?
Have you got a lot to do?

Short answers:

Are there many more (calls) to make?

Yes, (quite) a lot.	No, not (very) many.
Yes, lots.	No, not a lot.

Do you like it?

Yes, very much.	No, not (very) much.
Yes, (quite) a lot.	No, not a lot.

Some uses of *a few*, *a little* and *several*

Note that *a few* and *a little* mean *some*.
e.g. He made (quite) a few phone calls.
    Could I have a little milk, please?

Note that *few* and *little* mean *not many* and *not much*.
e.g. They have (very) few contacts in Poland.
    We have (very) little time.

Note that *several* means more than *some*, but less than *many*.
e.g. We have several contacts in Latin America.
    There are several good watch repairers in the area.

Note the following short answers.
e.g. Have you got any contacts there?
    Yes, several. / Yes, a few. / Yes, but very few.
    Have you got any free time?
    Yes, a little. / Yes, but very little.

Some uses of *so* and *such (a)*

Note the following examples of *so*.
e.g. Their products are so cheap that we
    can't compete.

There are so many points to remember.
There isn't so much pressure now.

Note the following examples of *such (a)*.
e.g. They have such good contacts that it's difficult to compete
    with them.
    It was such a big order that …

Some notes on time references

We use *at* with precise times.
e.g. at midnight   at two o'clock

Note also *at night*, *at the weekend*, *at Christmas*, *at lunchtime*.

We use *on* with days.
e.g. on the 4th of July   on Monday
    on Independence Day

We use *in* with other times.
e.g. in 2008   in the morning
    in the first quarter   in winter

We do not use a preposition with *today*, *tomorrow*, *yesterday*, *tonight*, etc.
e.g. I'll call you tomorrow.

We do not use a preposition with *next*, *last* and *this*.
e.g. They are coming this Saturday.
    I'll see you next week.

Useful phrases

Do you know any potential suppliers in the Poznan area?
There are a few I can recommend.   There are quite a lot.
Not very many.   Very few.
Do you have any other contacts in Poland?
Do you know anyone who supplies copiers?
Yes I do.   No, I'm afraid I don't.

We have a lot of contacts in Eastern Europe.
And I have a few very good contacts in Bulgaria.
I know several people who could help you.
I'm afraid we have very few contacts in that area.

What's your accountant like?
I can recommend her.
She's very efficient.
She's reliable and hard-working.
She's really good to work with.

Let me give you some other names and addresses.
I'll give you a letter of introduction.

AC is such a large company it's difficult to compete with it.
It's so efficient that we can't compete.

We met a couple of days ago.
last week   the week before last
Let's meet for lunch on the 10th.
in ten days time   a week on Monday
I'll see you then.   I look forward to it.

UNIT 3 Out of the office

1 Overview

Key dialogues

Listen to the conversations and answer the questions.

a Why is the man calling?
Why can't he get through?

b Is it possible to contact Mr Hanan?
Does Reception have a mobile number for him?

c Why did she miss him earlier?
What is the plan for the evening?

d Why is he late?
What time are the others arriving?

Preparation

Prepare to talk about how your organisation or other organisations you know handle calls out of office hours. Are calls switched through to mobile phones? Is there an emergency contact number?

Have you recently needed to contact someone and had problems doing so? What did you do?

Refer to the unit Language Notes and Useful Phrases on page 24.

2 Practice

Making contact outside working hours

In groups of three, practise making arrangements and meeting up. Use the table as a guide.

Partner A: You are working late.
Partner B: You are an outside caller. You want to speak to **Partner C**.
Partner C: You have already left the office.

Partner A takes an outside call from **Partner B**.

> I'm sorry, but I'm afraid the office is closed.
> You've missed him/her.
> He/She has gone home.
> Let me give you his/her mobile number.
> I'm afraid we don't give out mobile numbers.
> I'll try to get a message to him/her.

> Do you know how I can get in touch with [Fahad Morales]?
> Is it possible to get hold of him/her?
> Do you have his/her mobile number?
> Would you mind calling him/her?
> Would you ask him/her to phone me?

Partner C calls **Partner B**.

> I just got your message.
> Where are you?
> What's the problem?
> Are you coming this evening?
> How long will you be?

> I've been trying to contact you.
> My afternoon meeting has just finished.
> Your office wouldn't give me your number.
> I didn't know how to reach you.
> What's the address?
> I'll see you in about [20 minutes].

Partner C welcomes **Partner B**.

> You made it. It's good to see you.
> Come and meet ....
> Would you like a drink?
> What would you like?

> I'm sorry I'm so late.
> Good to meet you.
> It's been a long day.
> Just [some water] please.

Look at the examples in Language Notes (page 24) as you do these exercises.

Requests (can, could, would, etc.)

1 Change the demands into requests.

e.g. Ask her to call me.

  Could you ask her to call me?

a Write down this phone number down.

....

b Take this parcel to reception.

....

c Give her a message.

....

d Book my flight tickets.

....

e Don't give anyone my home number.

....

f Don't park there.

....

g Don't phone me tomorrow.

....

Offers (shall, let, can, etc.)

2 Offer to help, using the prompts.

e.g. (take a message)

  Can I take a message?

a (call you next week)

....

b (prepare an agenda for the meeting)

....

c (get in touch with the Beijing office)

....

d (book some theatre tickets for you)

....

e (buy you a drink)

....

f (drive you to the station)

....

g (check the order number)

....

3 With reference to the examples you have written and those in the Language Notes, practise making short requests and offers in pairs. Respond as indicated in the Language Notes examples.

Mobile phone/cell phone language

4 Complete the sentences with words from the box.

▶ line	▶ battery	▶ text
▶ message	▶ charger	▶ desk
▶ pick	▶ voice	▶ answer

a I couldn't .... my phone. I was in a meeting.

b The .... is very bad. I'll call you later.

c This is a .... for Kemal Rodriguez.

d I'll call you later. I'm not at my .... at the moment.

e Can you call me when you .... up this message.

f I'm sorry you couldn't contact me. My .... was flat.

g Do you have a spare .... ? I left mine at home.

h Please leave a message on my .... mail.

i .... me when you get to the airport.

4 Listening

Leaving messages

Listen and write down the voicemail messages.

a

Connected:

To: Rodney Vale

From: Joaquim Delgado – Medina Plastico

Message: Call between 2 and 5pm tomorrow.

MUTE   SPEAKER

b

Voice mailbox

To: ....

From: ....

Message: ....

Options   Exit

c

Voice mailbox

To: ....

From: ....

Message: ....

Options   Exit

d

To: ....

From: ....

Message: ....

MUTE   SPEAKER

5 Application

Contacting someone urgently

1 A fax arrives at Ergo Construction from the Commercial Investment Bank. Read it. Then listen to the conversation and answer the questions opposite. Why is the fax so urgent?

URGENT FAX MESSAGE!
PLEASE READ IMMEDIATELY!

I am trying to contact Tony Lopez, the head of your legal department, but your switchboard is closed and I do not have his direct number.

This is urgent as I am supposed to be meeting him for dinner at seven o'clock to discuss some important business, but I do not know the name or address of the restaurant.

If he is still in the building, could you ask him to contact me as soon as possible. If he has left, I would be very grateful if you could call and give me his home or mobile number. I am on 0203 437 294.

With thanks

Fiona Walker

Fiona Walker
Loans Manager

a Who calls Fiona Walker back?
b Does Ms Walker call Tony Lopez's home number?
c Where are they meeting?
d Why hasn't Ms Walker got the details?
e How will she get to the meeting place?

2 Send a message in which you ask someone to contact you urgently.

LANGUAGE REFERENCE

Language notes

For more detailed notes, see the Business Grammar Guide.

Requests

Can/could I make a booking?
Could/would you tell him I called (please)?
   Yes, of course. / No problem.
Could/would you (please) not tell him?
   Yes, of course. / No problem.
Could he/she call me on this number?
Would you mind giving me a lift?
   No, of course not. / No problem.
Would you mind not smoking (please)?
   No, of course not. / No problem.

Please is often used in simple polite requests.
e.g. Please call me.
     Please don't call me between 3 and 4pm.
     Please let me know as soon as possible.
     Please could/would you send me a copy?
     Could/would you please look into this matter?

We can also use:
I would be very grateful if you could call me.

Offers

Offering something:
Can/could I get you something to drink?
Yes, I'd love a coffee.   No, I'm fine thanks.

Offering to do something:
Shall I open the window?
   Yes, please. It's very hot in here.
   If you don't mind, I'd rather you didn't.
Would you like me to send you a copy?
   Yes, please.   No it's OK. I've already
                      got one.
Let me help you.
   Thanks very much. It's OK thanks. I can manage.

Using your mobile phone

Can you speak?
Can you speak up? (= *Can you speak louder?*)
I'm in a meeting.
I'm not at my desk.
I'll call you back in five minutes.
Sorry, I can't hear you.
Reception is very bad.
My battery is nearly flat.
This is a message for Jan Picker.
I'll check my voicemail later.
Sorry to cut you off earlier.
I had to switch my phone off.

Useful phrases

I'm trying to contact Toria Noritz.
Do you know how I can get in touch with her?
Is it possible to contact her on this number?
Where can I get hold of her?

I'm meeting Saleh this evening.
We're going out to dinner.
Do you have his number?

I'm afraid the office is closed.
He has already gone home.
I'm afraid we don't give out private numbers.

Shall I ask him to call you in the morning?
Would you like me to get a message to him?
Let me get him to call you.

Would you ask him to phone me, please?
Could you give him a message?
Yes, of course.
Would you mind calling back tomorrow?
No problem.

I've been trying to contact you.
I didn't know how to reach you.
Your mobile was switched off.

It's good to see you again.
It's good to be here.
I'm glad you made it.

This is a message for Fiona.
Hi, it's Peter. It's about next Friday.
I'll be on my mobile all afternoon.
I'll try and call you again later.

UNIT 4 Introducing your company

Preparation

Bring to the lesson as many of the following as possible: company organisation charts, company brochures, annual reports, maps showing company locations and layouts. This information will be referred to throughout the unit.

If you do not work for a company, bring background information about companies which are of interest to you.

Refer to the unit Language Notes and Useful Phrases on page 28.

1 Overview

Key dialogues

Listen to the dialogues and answer the questions.

a What kind of company is it?
What are its main activities?
b What is Tommy Hoe's position?
Is the R&D section responsible for product development?
c Where is their production based?
Where is the head office?
d Is the site near Hinton?
How do you get to the office once you are in the main building?

2 Practice

Refer to the Language Notes on page 28.

Describing location and layout

1 Work in pairs. Find out the location of your partner's company. Where is it? How do you get there?

2 Describe the layout of your company to your partner.

Useful language

in the north of [the country]
south of [the river]
on the coast
to the west of [the town]
not far from [Guangzhou]
about 50 kilometres north-east of [Recife]
(right) in the centre of town
on/off [the ringroad]
just outside a place called [Mexian]

Useful language

over there
across [the car park]
(on) the other side of [that building]
to the left/right of
on the [second] floor
at the top/bottom of the stairs
at the end of the corridor
the [third] door on the left/right

3 Language focus

High numbers

1 In how many ways can you say these figures? Refer to the Language Notes on page 28.

a	0.25m	**c**	0.5m	**e**	0.75bn	**g**	1,276,005
b	1.25m	**d**	3.5m	**f**	3.75bn	**h**	7,370,565,725

Vocabulary building

2 Complete the sentences with words from the box below. Use the singular or plural form. Then write sentences about your own company or one which you know using these words.

> ▶ subsidiary ▶ client ▶ acquisition
> ▶ activity ▶ turnover ✓ ▶ employee
> ▶ supplier ▶ profit ▶ sale

e.g. Our annual _turnover_ is £3.5m.

a We have 500 .... in our London plant.
b Our main .... are in manufacturing.
c Last year, we made £$^1/_2$m ....
d We made an important .... in Australia last year.
e We now have .... in ten countries.
f We try to keep our .... happy by offering a good service.
g We insist that all of our .... are accredited.
h .... are better than they have ever been.

4 Listening

Basic company information

1 Listen to the conversation, and fill in the form.
2 Fill in the form on page 133 for you and your company. Change the currency as necessary.

1 Name

Title ____ First name _____ Surname _____
Position _____
Business name _____
Business address _____
_____ Postcode/Zipcode _____
Telephone number _____

2 Type of business

Sole proprietor	☐	PLC	☐
Partnership	☐	Subsidiary	☐
Private Limited Company	☐	Other	☐

3 Turnover

Up to £250,000	☐	£5m–20m	☐
£250,000–£5m	☐	£20m+	☐

4 Currently involved in import/export

Export only	☐	Import and export	☐
Import only	☐	None	☐

5 Number of employees

1–30	☐	101–500	☐
31–100	☐	501+	☐

6 Your company's main business activities

Agriculture, forestry and fishing	☐
Energy and water supply	☐
Mining, chemicals	☐
Metal goods, engineering, vehicles	☐
Electronics	☐
Other manufacturing industries	☐
Construction	☐
Retail, distribution, hotels, catering, repairs	☐
Transport, communications	☐
Banking, financial, business services	☐
Education, health, government and local authorities	☐
Other	☐

Company background information

1 Work with a partner. Find out about the organisation which he/she works for, using the following headings.

- Type of company
- Main markets
- Annual turnover
- Profitability
- Number of employees
- Location of offices, plants, etc.
- Main products or services
- Location of parent company

2 How does this organisation chart compare with yours? Describe the organisation of your company/business unit/organisation to a partner. Use any charts which you have brought to class.

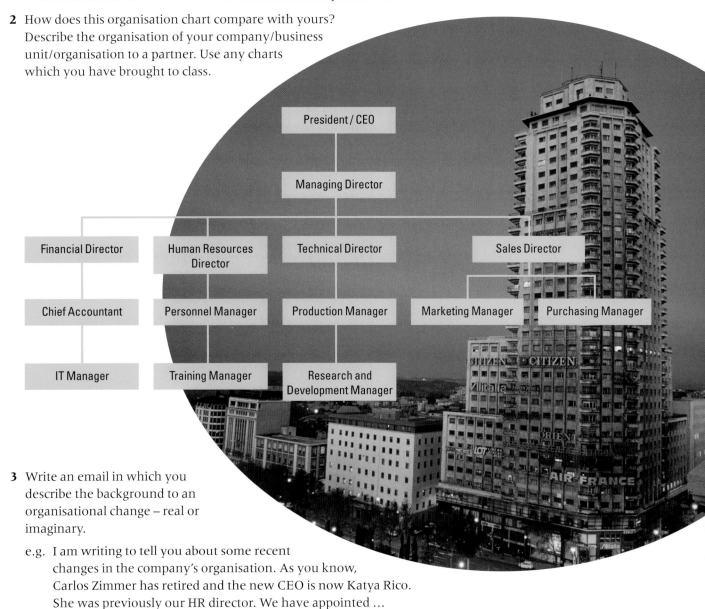

3 Write an email in which you describe the background to an organisational change – real or imaginary.

e.g. I am writing to tell you about some recent changes in the company's organisation. As you know, Carlos Zimmer has retired and the new CEO is now Katya Rico. She was previously our HR director. We have appointed …

LANGUAGE REFERENCE

Language notes

For more detailed notes, see the Business Grammar Guide.

High numbers

Note how you say the following:

100,000	a / one hundred thousand
150,000	a / one hundred and fifty thousand
23,500,000	twenty-three million five hundred thousand
250,000	a quarter of a million / two hundred and fifty thousand
500,000	half a million / five hundred thousand
750,000	three-quarters of a million / seven hundred and fifty thousand
3,250,000	three and a quarter million / three point two five million / three million two hundred and fifty thousand
3.75m	three and three-quarter million / three point seven five million / three million seven hundred and fifty thousand
2.5bn	two and a half billion / two point five billion
5.82bn	five point eight two billion

Abbreviations:

20k = twenty thousand
70m = seventy million
2bn = two billion

Geographical location

It's **(to the) south of** London.
It's **in the north of** the country.
It's **500km north-west of** Beijing.
It's **just outside** Frankfurt.
It's **on** the coast / **inland**.
It's **just off** the motorway.
It's **on** a main road.
It's **in** the centre/middle of the city.
It's **in** an industrial zone / **on** an industrial estate.
It's **in** the suburbs.
It's **near** / **not far from** / **close to** the centre.
It's **surrounded by** hills.

It's **beyond** the car park.
It's **on the other side of** that building.

Location inside a building

It's **to the left/right of** the lift.
It's **on** the ground floor.
It's **at the top/bottom** of the stairs.
It's **at the end of the** corridor.
It's **across** the corridor.
It's **the second door on the left/right**.

Useful phrases

What type of company is it?
It's a public limited company.
They make electronic sensors.
They're in the export business.

The company has three divisions.
Tommy Hoe is the chief accountant.
He reports to the finance director.
Tommy has a staff of 12.

My company is based in Sweden.
We're on the east coast.
Our head office isn't far from Stockholm.

Our main European factory is about 70 kilometres east of Brussels.
It's outside a place called Bruges.
It's just off the ring road.
It will take you two hours to drive there.

Excuse me, where is the main office?
Can you tell me how to get to the warehouse?

The warehouse is behind the administration block.
The training department is on the third floor.
My office is on the other side of the building.
It's at the end of the corridor.
If you get lost, just ask someone!

Our annual turnover is approximately $2.5 million.
Zodamot's sales are just over €3.5 million.
In comparison, Nabiko's worldwide sales are over ¥1.2 billion.

UNIT 5 Company profiles

1 Overview

Key dialogues

Listen and answer the questions.

a What kind of company is SEW?
Does it receive any subsidies?

b Is NPC a nationalised industry? What does it do?

c When was the company founded?
Is it still state-owned?

d What is the man's job?
What is he working on at the moment?

Preparation

Prepare to describe some well-known companies in your country. You could focus on the public utilities (water, electricity, gas, nuclear power, etc.).

How are these companies owned? Are they privately owned, state monopolies? Are they private companies with major state shareholding? (etc.)

Refer to page 32, and study the Language Notes and Useful Phrases for this unit.

2 Practice

A brief company description

1 Read the text. Describe the company's position in the market. Then find phrases in the text which have a similar meanings to the following.

a brought into state ownership ....
b make use of ....
c facilities ....
d represented ....
e additional ....
f purchases ....
g only ....

2 Give a brief description of one of the companies which you have researched.

A law was passed in June 1982, which created XLD as a state company. Most of the electricity production and distribution companies that existed at that time were nationalised. The same law gave XLD a monopoly over the transmission, distribution, import and export of electricity.

However, the law allowed other companies to own and exploit production units to cover their own electricity needs, provided they sold excess production exclusively to XLD.

As a result, XLD buys in some of its production from other electricity producers. Last year, XLD production accounted for 94% of the electricity produced in the country, whereas sales accounted for 97% of electricity consumption.

Check the Language Notes on page 32 as you do these exercises.

The Simple Present vs. the Present Continuous

1 Write the verbs in the simple or continuous form.

e.g. The company .**manufactures**. (manufacture) components for the car industry.

a I .... (forget) the name of the company.

b It .... (have) turnover of $10m.

c It .... (suffer) from the effects of the recession.

d It .... (make) a loss.

e What .... (you) (do) with the photocopier?

f I .... (try) to mend it.

g If our clients .... (consider) moving, we .... (provide) assistance.

h If companies .... (think) of relocating, we .... (give) advice.

Verbs normally used in the Simple Present

2 Note that the verbs below are normally used in the simple form. Complete the sentences.

e.g. I hear ....**that XLD are opening a new power plant.**............ .

a I believe ....

b We don't own ....

c I hear ....

d I (can) smell ....

e I think I know ....

f I know ....

g I feel ....

h That .... belongs to me.

make *and* do

3 Complete these phrases with *make* or *do*. Use a dictionary to help you. Then use the phrases in sentences which you might use in your everyday work.

e.g. I haven't made a decision about when to hold the meeting.

a .... a decision (about)

b .... very well (with)

c .... a lot of work (for)

d .... plans

e .... better/worse (than)

f .... money/a profit

g .... business (with)

h .... notes (on)

i .... some filing

j .... a point (about)

k .... something/nothing (about)

l .... an effort (to)

A public utility company

1 Listen to the interview with an employee of a major European energy supplier as she gives an overview of the company. What is her job? Tick the categories below that she discusses.

Type of company	☐	Market position	☐	Main site(s)	☐
History	☐	Customer base	☐	Turnover	☐
Main activities	☐	Number of employees	☐	Profit	☐

2 Read the key facts and figures about Vattenfall, a major European energy company. How does this company compare with the companies which you are familiar with? Check Vattenfall's international website (www.vattenfall.com).

KEY FACTS AND FIGURES

Vattenfall at a glance

Vattenfall acts in all parts of the electricity value chain – generation, transmission, distribution and sales. We are also active in electricity trading, and we generate, distribute and sell heat.

Vattenfall is Europe's fifth largest generator of electricity and the largest generator of heat. Our vision is to be a leading European energy company.

Vattenfall currently has operations in Sweden, Finland, Germany and Poland. The parent company, Vattenfall AB, is wholly owned by the Swedish state.

Vattenfall facts and figures

33,017 employees at time of writing

Electricity sales: 186.4TWh per year

Electricity generation: 167.1TWh per year

Heat production and sales: 34.5TWh per year

Key figures for the fiscal year

Net sales: SEK113.4 billion (€12.6bn)

Investments: SEK12.6 billion (€1.4bn)

SEK = Swedish krona
TWh = a terawatt hour (a measurement of energy)

LANGUAGE REFERENCE

Language notes

For more detailed notes, see the Business Grammar Guide.

Some expressions of state involvement

It's a state-owned company.
It's a public utility.
It's a state monopoly.
It's owned by the state/government.
It's subsidised by the state/government.
It was nationalised/privatised in 2003.

Simple Present vs. Present Continuous

We use the Present Simple to talk about:
– permanent features and things that happen on a regular basis
e.g. My brother **is** a lawyer.
      The factory **makes** aircraft components.
      What **does** your company **do**?

– timetables and events
e.g. The display **begins at** 10am.

We use the Present Continuous to talk about:
– things that are happening at the moment of speaking
e.g. – What **are** you **doing**?
      – I'm **working** on my report.

– situations that are temporary, happening around the present time or developing trends
e.g. I'm **working** on an interesting project.
      How **is** the business **doing**?
      Prices **are going up** all the time?

Verbs normally used in the Present Simple

The Present Simple is usually used with state verbs:
– verbs of thinking and knowing (e.g. *believe*, *think* (= *believe*), *agree*, *understand*, *know*, *remember*, *forget*, *realise*, *expect*, etc.)
e.g. I **think** that's a great idea.
      I **agree**.
      I **expect** he'll be tired when he arrives.

– verbs of feeling or preference (e.g. *want*, *wish*, *like*, *hate*, *matter*, *mind*, etc.)
e.g. The company **wants** to relocate.
      I **don't mind** where we go.

– verbs of perception (*taste*, *hear*, *see*, *smell*, etc.)
e.g. This coffee **tastes** awful.
      Can you **smell** burning?
      (Note: these verbs are often used with *can*.)

– verbs of possession (e.g. *have got*, *own*, *belong*, etc.)
e.g. Who **does** this jacket **belong** to?
      They **have** sales offices all over the world.

Useful phrases

I work for a power company.
I believe it's state owned.
I think it's publicly owned.
It's a public utility company.

Does the company receive subsidies?
Is it subsidised?
It receives substantial government subsidies.
Although it's a state monopoly, it's run like a private company.

What are your main business activities?
Where are your main sites?
How many people do you employ?
Where are your main markets?

Basically, we make and distribute electricity.
We operate a number of power stations.
  gas works   water works
  sewage plants   coal mines
We are the world's largest producer of electricity.
We account for 94% of the electricity produced in the country.

I believe we are the largest producer of gas in the region.
We are the market leaders.

And what do you do in the company?
What's your job?   What's your position?
I'm an engineer, but I work as a project manager.
Currently, I'm working in Algeria.

MBV do a lot of business with gas companies.
They make very good profits.

UNIT 6 Competitors

1 | Overview

Key dialogues

Listen to the dialogues and answer the questions.

a Does this recruitment consultancy have much competition?
Are their competitors more or less profitable than them?

b How does SAL compete with Cosmar and Rowdell?
What is Cosmar's position in the US market?

c What is the competition like in the domestic market?
What is KLT's position in several Middle Eastern countries?

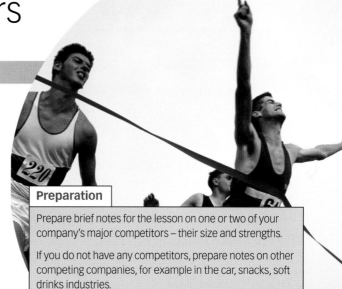

Preparation

Prepare brief notes for the lesson on one or two of your company's major competitors – their size and strengths.

If you do not have any competitors, prepare notes on other competing companies, for example in the car, snacks, soft drinks industries.

Refer to the Language Reference section for this unit on page 36.

2 | Talking point

Beating the competition

Read 'Hot tips for beating the competition'. Which tips do you agree with?
Do you find any of the suggestions unethical? There are five more 'hot tips' on page 133.
What do you think they might be?

Hot tips for beating the competition

BY ERIC GILBOORD
(adapted from *Canadaone* magazine)

1 Know what you want. Be clear about the information you are looking for. Much of what you are seeking is readily available. Talk to your staff, customers and suppliers. Go out equipped with a list of the specific information you require. Look for the competitors' price plans, additional services and staff capabilities. Review their product line and determine how much overlap there is with your own offerings.

2 Get to know your competitors. Make sure you balance older established businesses with ones new to the market. Talk to them at trade shows when they are more inclined to be chatty. But be cautious; as a sharp competitor they may feed you misinformation or embellish sales figures to make themselves look good.

3 Make competitive links. If you have many competitors, put the information on a spreadsheet. Look for the common themes of successful and unsuccessful competitors. Overall, try to determine their individual strategies. Don't be surprised if several share the same strategy.

4 Use the Internet. Use the Internet for a quick insight into a competitor. The information is freely available and easily accessible. As a starting point, find out whether your competitors have a website and review it thoroughly. Look at association or industry-specific sites for upcoming trends in your area of business.

5 Contact your competitors. Call or visit competitors, both direct and indirect (related businesses), and talk to their staff. Employees can unwittingly be tremendous sources of valuable information. You may need to make several calls or visits to develop a complete picture.

As you do these exercises, look at the unit Language Notes on page 36.

Comparative and superlative adjectives

1 Answer the questions. Work in pairs. Refer to your preparation notes.

a Can you think of a company which is smaller than yours?

b … and one that has a higher turnover?

c Can you think of any jobs which would be more interesting than yours?

d … and any which would be less interesting?

e Is job satisfaction more or less important than job security?

f What is the most enjoyable meal you have ever had?

g … and the least enjoyable?

2 Read these statements. Number the companies in order of size, from ⬚1⬚ to ⬚6⬚.

a Company A is by far the biggest. ⬚1⬚

b Company B is about the same size as Company C. ⬚

c Company C is slightly bigger than Company B. ⬚

d Company D is a little smaller than Company B. ⬚

e Company E is the smallest company. ⬚

f Company F is far bigger than Company E, but smaller than all of the other companies. ⬚

Geographical areas

3 Give the names of countries in these areas. Make use of an atlas to help you. Then add the related nationalities.

e.g. Europe: ...... *Bulgaria, Switzerland* ......
Nationalities: ...... *Bulgarians, Swiss* ......

a Latin America: ....
Nationalities: ....

b Far East: ....
Nationalities: ....

c North Africa: ....
Nationalities: ....

d Middle East: ....
Nationalities: ....

e Central America: ....
Nationalities: ....

f Other areas: ....
Nationalities: ....

Expressing opinions

4 In pairs, compare what you think about:

- making negative comments about the competition
- industrial piracy
- protectionist policies
- segregated staff dining-rooms
- company cars and other benefits.

e.g. – What do you think about making negative comments about competitors?
 – I don't agree with it. I don't believe it helps you to sell your products.

> **Useful language**
>
> What do you think?
> What's your opinion?
> Do you agree with me?
> You agree with me, don't you?
> I (don't) think/believe …
> I (don't) consider that …
> In my opinion/view …
> I'm (not) convinced that …

4 | Listening

Talking about the competition

Listen, and match the companies with the competition they face.

a A toy manufacturer
b A mining company
c A machinery manufacturer
d A firm of solicitors
e A construction company

i   Competition coming from South-East Asia
ii   No competition
iii Hard competition
iv   Facing hard price competition
v   Almost no competition at the moment

5 | Application

Comparing companies

1 Read the Magnol press release below. Then find words in the text that have the same meaning as the following.

a expertise ....
b which employs ....
c shares or investment ....
d stressed ....
e ensures ....
f raises ....

2 Omega Laminating Ltd, Magnol's competitor, has recently opened a new factory. Study the notes on Omega below. Then, in pairs, discuss the differences between Magnol and Omega.

Notes on Omega Laminating Ltd

New factory opened in Backtown, end of last year

Company owned by the Fordex family

2 laminating lines

Investment cost: €2.5m

200 people employed

Annual production capacity: 15,000 tonnes of laminated material per year

Annual turnover to June: €10 million

Background: The Fordex family have operated a factory in Backtown for over 100 years. They are specialists in laminating and this factory replaces their old factory, which was destroyed by a fire two years ago.

MAGNOL
PRESS RELEASE

Not to be released until 10am, 13 March

A new laminating line has been completed at the Magnol Laminator factory in Arls. This €2.5m investment makes the factory the most technologically advanced in Europe, and guarantees continued production at the factory employing 120 people.

The new line increases the factory's annual production capacity to 25,000 tonnes of laminated material.

Magnol's annual turnover is approximately €16m. The managing director is Mr Bertrand Rosen and the chairman of the Board of Directors is Mr Harry Lam.

The Arls factory has a history of more than 40 years of laminating various materials. Two years ago, Magnol became a subsidiary of the Japanese AMP Corporation. AMP is a diversified company with major interests in shipping machinery and construction.

In his speech at the opening ceremony, Mr Sei Iwamura emphasised that Magnol Laminators is an excellent example of the collaboration between Japanese 'know-how' and local skills.

Useful language

How does the [annual production] compare?
What about [turnover]?
What are the [investment] figures?
Do you know who owns the companies?
Do you know anything about the history of the companies?
Magnol have a great production capacity.
Omega are probably more specialised.
Magnol are part of a larger group, etc.

LANGUAGE REFERENCE

Language notes

For more detailed notes, see the Business Grammar Guide.

Comparative and superlative adjectives

Short adjectives:
short, shorter, shortest
large, larger, largest
big, bigger, biggest

Longer adjectives:
expensive, more expensive, most expensive
less expensive, least expensive

Irregular adjectives:
good, better, best
bad, worse, worst
far, farther (further), farthest (furthest)
little, less, least
much, more, most

Examples:
Their subsidy is (much) larger than ours.
It's (far) more profitable than it was.
It's (not) the most important development.
It's the best alternative.
This job is (much) less interesting than my last one.
Size is the least important factor in this market.
We're (not) as well established as you are.

Expressing opinions

Asking for opinions:
What do you think?
What do you think of the new marketing manager?
    (*of* + person/thing)
What do you think about the proposed cuts?
    (*about* + situation)
What's your opinion/view (on this)?
Do you agree with me?
Do you consider it's worth doing?

Giving opinions:
I (don't) think it's a good idea.
In my opinion/view …
I reckon …

Useful phrases

We specialise in mail order.
We're more profitable than our competitors.
We're the most profitable company in Italy.
Our competitors are far less profitable.
Their prices are higher.
They have fewer customers than us.

We offer a better service than our competitors.
The quality of our products is far higher.
Our sales network is much better.
In my view, price is the most important factor.
What is the least important factor?

What's your opinion? What do you think?
I think that the location of a business is vital.
I agree. I don't agree.
I don't think that's true.
Customers want the best quality at the cheapest price.

We consider ourselves to be the best in the business.
We're one of the largest producers in Asia.
We rank in the top ten companies worldwide.
We have a very strong market position.

The competition in our business is very hard.
We face tough competition.
The European market is so difficult that we can't compete.
We need to be more competitive.

We can't compete on price.
Our competitors' wage costs are lower.
Their supply chain is more streamlined.

UNIT 7 Your personal background

1 | Overview

Key dialogues

Listen to the conversations and answer the questions.

a What kind of job does the man have at the moment?
Does he have any children?

b Has Omar Marat retired?
Why doesn't the speaker like the summer?

c Who does he work for?
Is he married?

d What's wrong with her husband?
What kind of holiday were they planning?

Preparation

Come to the lesson prepared to talk about yourself, your family, your working life and your outside interests.

You may like to bring along some photos of yourself, your family, your leisure activities and even your pets!

Refer to the unit Language Notes and Useful Phrases on page 40.

2 | Practice

Personal background

1 Write questions using the prompts. Then ask a partner about him/herself.

e.g. where – born? *Where were you born?*

a still – live – there?

....

b where – live – now?

....

c house – apartment?

....

d married? in a relationship?

....

e children? grandchildren?

....

f boys? girls?

....

g ages?

....

h where – go – school, college, university, etc.?

....

i what – do – free time?

....

2 Introduce a fellow student to the rest of the group.

e.g. Helen was born in Athens, but she now lives on the Island of Kos.
She lives in a beautiful two-bedroom apartment, which overlooks the harbour …

Refer to the Language Notes on page 40 as you complete these exercises.

The Present Perfect tense

1 Read the sentences, then write another example in the Present Perfect tense. Use the prompts.

e.g. Have you ever worked in advertising?

(ever play) _Have you ever played basketball?_

a How long have you worked for CAB TV?
(live) ....

b House prices have increased this year.
(fall) ....

c The chairperson has resigned.
(retire) ....

d I have just seen your son.
(just meet) ....

e The clients haven't replied yet.
(call/yet) ....

f I still haven't decided what to do.
(still make up his mind) ....

2 In pairs, practise using the Present Perfect tense. Talk about the following.

Experiences
e.g. – Have you ever worked in …?
– No, never. / Yes, a long time ago.

The unfinished past
e.g. – How long have you been here?
– Since June. / For two years.

Developments
e.g. – We've expanded greatly in the last year.
– Yes, I know. / That's good.

News
e.g. – TLK have closed down.
– Really? When did that happen?

Current information
e.g. – I haven't completed my report yet.
– Why's that? / When do you think you will?

have to and had to

3 Match the questions in the box with the statements and questions below. Then, with a partner, discuss the things you have had to do.

HAVE YOU …

a … ever had to catch the 6am shuttle?

b … ever had to m-m-make a speech?

c … ever been stuck in a suit when it's 80 degrees in the shade?

d … ever had to fire someone?

e … ever been misquoted by a trade journalist?

f … ever had to cancel a holiday?

g … ever worked so late you've slept in the office?

Adapted from an advert for an insurance company which aims to be 'the choice of the professional'

i I mustn't forget to set my alarm clock!

ii I can't get away; something unexpected has come up.

iii Ladies and gentlemen …

iv Luckily, there's a comfortable sofa in my office.

v Is it always as hot as this?

vi I'm very sorry to have to tell you …

vii I'm sure I didn't say that.

4 Application

Personal news

1 Two people meet by chance and exchange news. Do they know each other well? Listen to the conversation and underline the words in the boxes which relate to Tom, the main speaker. 'Collecting antiques', for example, is underlined.

2 Working in pairs, practise exchanging personal news. Use the vocabulary in the boxes as a guide.

Work

clerical/manual worker
director, manager, sales executive
self-employed, unemployed
retired, made redundant
full-time/part-time employment

Interests

collecting antiques/coins
playing cards/football
reading, watching TV
skiing, boating, walking, golf
cookery, gardening, DIY
theatre, cinema, concerts

Health

in good health, well
back pain, arthritis
asthma, hay fever
sinus/heart trouble
headaches/migraine

Accommodation

a detached/semi-detached/
  terraced house
an apartment, a maisonette,
  a bungalow
purpose built/converted

LANGUAGE REFERENCE

Language notes

For more detailed notes, see the Business Grammar Guide.

The Present Perfect tense

Affirmative:

I have (I've) finished the job.
He has (He's) resigned.

Negative:

I have not (haven't) decide yet.
She has not (hasn't) changed her mind.

Interrogative:

What have you done about …?
Has he finished the work yet?

Short answers:

Yes, I have.　　No, I haven't.
Yes, he has.　　No, he hasn't.

Examples:

We have been here an hour (and we're still waiting).
I have been in sales all my life.
Have you done this sort of work before?
They've never been to Egypt.
The situation hasn't changed much since yesterday.

Some examples of *have to* and *have/had to*

Present:

I often have to speak English on the phone.
Do you ever have to work on Saturdays?
He doesn't have to reply till tomorrow.
I have to call my office.
We have to improve our security.

Past:

I often had to speak French with customers.
We had to change our suppliers.
Did you ever have to work at night?
He didn't have to pay the full price.

Useful phrases

I was born in the south of Spain.
Where do you live now?
In a small village 20 kilometres from Madrid.
We have a house in the middle of the village.
It's a terraced house.
How long have you lived there?

Are you married?
Do you have any children?
Yes, I have three children – two boys and a girl.
They're still at school.
My daughter is the oldest. She's 14.

What are you doing these days?
Are you still in the food industry?
Yes, but I'm not working full time.
I work part time.
Do you still work for Danilo?
Hasn't he retired yet?

Have you ever been self-employed?
Have you ever had to cancel a holiday?
Have you ever had to fire someone?
No, never.　　Yes, but it was a long time ago.

What do you do in your free time?
I spend most of my time gardening.
I prefer being outside.
I'm not very keen on watching TV.

How have you been recently?
Very well.
I've had a bad back.
I've been off work.
I've been in hospital.
I'm sorry to hear that.

UNIT 8 Conditions of work

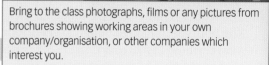

1 Overview

Key dialogues

Listen to the conversations and answer the questions.

a Does he have a company car?
  What clothing allowances do company employees receive?
b What was the first speaker doing when the fire started?
  Had the second speaker left the building when she phoned?
c What is the lighting in the office like?
  What about noise?

2 Practice

Office equipment and furniture

Preparation

Bring to the class photographs, films or any pictures from brochures showing working areas in your own company/organisation, or other companies which interest you.

Prepare to describe the images you bring into the class or to describe working environments which you know.

Look at the Language Reference section for this unit on page 44.

1 Match these captions with the numbered boxes in the diagram.

a Adequate lighting
b Table lamp: not too bright, no glare or distracting reflections
c Forearms approximately horizontal
d Adjustable seat back
e Screen, stable image, adjustable, readable, glare- and reflection-free
f Good back support
g Window covering
h Adjustable seat height
i Leg room: enough space to allow user to change position

j No excess pressure on backs of thighs and backs of knees
k Work surface: spacious, glare-free, allowing flexible arrangements
l Software: appropriate to task, adapted to user
m Keyboard: usable, adjustable, detachable, legible
n Foot support if needed

2 Describe your own working environment. Is it comfortable? How could it be improved?

3 Language focus

Check the Language Notes on page 44 as you complete these exercises.

too/enough

1 In pairs, discuss your working environment. Use *too/enough* as appropriate.

   e.g. Is it comfortable to work in?

   Is there enough space for everyone?

   It is quiet enough (for you to be able to concentrate)?

   Is the lighting bright enough (for you not to strain your eyes)?

   The office is too noisy for me to concentrate.

   The work isn't interesting enough for me.

   The hours aren't long enough to get through everything I have to do.

   There is certainly enough storage space.

The Past Continuous tense

2 Practise using the Past Continuous tense.

   e.g. I was talking to a client when the fire started.

   Ask a partner questions from the table. Write down his/her replies.

Where were you living	this time last year/month?
Where were you working	on Tuesday morning?
What were you doing	at 2pm on Friday?
What were you working on	between three and four yesterday?

3 Listen to the following people talking about a fire in their office. Tick the ones who were still in the building. What were they all doing at the time?

Sofia ☐ ....
....

Mona ☐ ....
....

Andrew ☐ ....
....

Khalid ☐ ....
....

The Past Perfect tense

4 Put the verbs in brackets into either the Simple Past (*did*) or the Past Perfect tense (*had done*).

   e.g. I left the building when the fire started.
      I had already left the building when the fire started.

   a I .... (ask) Maria Sanchez to join us for dinner yesterday.

   b Unfortunately, she .... (arrange) to be somewhere else.

   c She .... (call) me last night.

   d She said she .... (try) to change her arrangements …

   e … but it .... (not be) possible.

   f She .... (not know) you were coming.

   g She .... (want) to meet you very much.

   h I tried to call you, but you .... (leave) the office.

4 Listening

Perks and benefits

1 Listen and tick the benefits offered by the speakers' companies.

	Sp 1	Sp 2	Sp 3
subsidised housing			
free school for children			
sports facilities			
a company car			
a subsidised canteen			
discount prices on company products			
bonus			
clothing allowance			
pension			
low-interest loans			
health insurance			
health insurance for family			
life insurance			
a weighting allowance			

5 Application

Comparing benefits

1 In pairs, complete the chart of benefits enjoyed by a UK company's employees.

Partner A: Your information is below.
Partner B: Your information is on page 134.

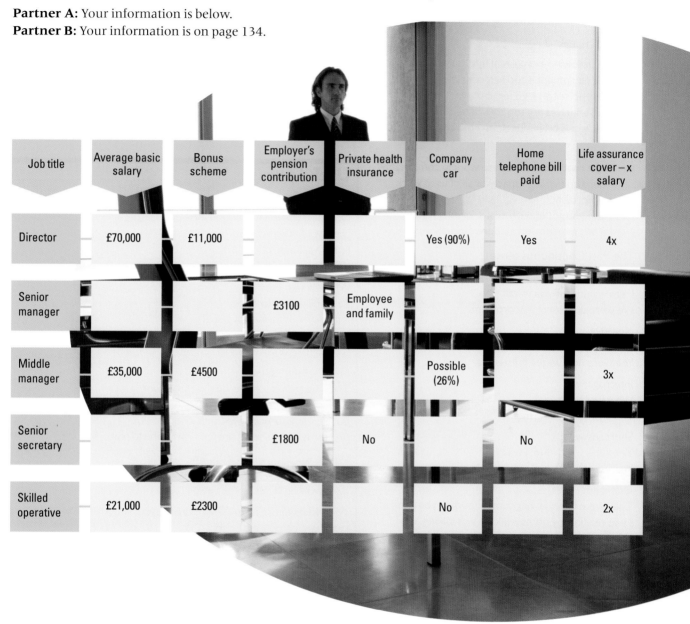

Job title	Average basic salary	Bonus scheme	Employer's pension contribution	Private health insurance	Company car	Home telephone bill paid	Life assurance cover – x salary
Director	£70,000	£11,000			Yes (90%)	Yes	4x
Senior manager			£3100	Employee and family			
Middle manager	£35,000	£4500			Possible (26%)		3x
Senior secretary			£1800	No		No	
Skilled operative	£21,000	£2300			No		2x

2 How do these benefits compare with those in your company/country?
Do you enjoy any other benefits which are not mentioned here?

> **Useful language**
>
> What is a [director's] basic salary?
> Does he/she get private health insurance?
> What does it cover?
> Does the company pay his/her phone bill?
> Is there a bonus scheme?
> What is the scheme worth?

LANGUAGE REFERENCE

Language notes

For more detailed notes, see the Business Grammar Guide.

too and enough

Note the following examples of *too*.

e.g. This equipment is too heavy for me to lift.

Is the noise too loud for you?

These shelves are too high to reach.

The light is bright, but it isn't too bright.

Note the following examples of *enough*.

e.g. Is the room cool enough to work in comfortably?

There isn't enough space for all of us to work comfortably.

Have you got enough chairs for everyone?

I didn't read the instructions carefully enough.

The Past Continuous tense

Affirmative:

I was waiting for you to call.

We were discussing that problem.

Negative:

It was not (wasn't) working.

You were not (weren't) listening.

Interrogative:

What was he saying?

Were you expecting me?

Short answers:

Yes, I was.   No, I wasn't.

Yes, we were.   No, we weren't.

Examples:

They were interviewing someone when you phoned.

I was reading my notes while he was talking.

Where were you working this time last year?

The Past Perfect tense

Affirmative:

We had (We'd) gone home by then.

She had (She'd) already told us that …

Negative:

I had not (hadn't) expected the job to be …

They had not (hadn't) started when …

Interrogative:

Had the meeting ended by the time you …?

Had he begun his new job by then?

Short answers:

Yes, it had.   No, it hadn't.

Yes, you had.   No, you hadn't.

Examples:

I thought that you'd made a decision.

When I went down to reception, the visitor had already left.

Had we moved to the new offices when you joined the company?

Useful phrases

What benefits do you receive in your job?

Do you get private health insurance?

Does your company pay your phone bill?

Is there a bonus scheme?

What's the scheme worth?

What's your office like?

Is it a good place to work?

Is it noisy?   Is it a friendly place?

Is there enough space for everyone?

Is the lighting bright enough?

There's plenty of space.

The lighting is reasonable – it's not too bright.

The office chairs are very comfortable.

But the work surfaces aren't wide enough.

And some of the shelves are too high for me to reach.

Where were you working this time last year?

What were you working on?

I was working in Pisa on the Dexo project.

What were you doing between three and four o'clock this afternoon?

I was having a very late lunch.

I was making some coffee when the alarm went off.

When I got outside, smoke was coming out of the window.

I had just finished work.

I tried to call you, but you had already gone home.

UNIT 9 Job descriptions

1 Overview

Key dialogues

Listen to the exchanges and answer the questions.

a What experience does the new finance director have? What is her educational background?

b Why does the speaker spend so much time in meetings? Does the job involve financial planning?

c Why does he recommend the job candidate? What relevant experience has she had?

Preparation

Bring to the class any job advertisements that are used in your fields, and/or CVs which you have access to, with names and details blanked out.

Be prepared to describe your own job in detail and others described in the job advertisements. Compare these with your 'ideal job'.

Refer to the unit Language Notes and Useful Phrases on page 48.

2 Practice

Your previous job

1 Find out about the previous jobs which your fellow learners have had. Refer to the questions and Useful Phrases (page 48) as necessary. Take notes.

> Why did you take the job?
> What did the job involve?
> What did you have to do?
> What special skills did you need?
> What did you like/dislike about it?
> What was the most difficult/challenging aspect of it?
> Did you have any problems?
> What were your colleagues like?

2 Refer to your notes and introduce your colleagues to the rest of the group.

e.g. Maria has worked in the retail industry for 15 years. She worked for three years in sales, which involved …

Check the Language Notes on page 48 as you do these exercises.

Replying to negative sentences

1 In pairs, practise confirming negative sentences.

e.g. So you aren't responsible for [logistics]?

No, I'm not.

a You don't speak [Spanish], (do you?)

....

b They haven't finished yet, (have they?)

....

c So you can't make the meeting.

....

d They didn't phone, (did they?)

....

e You wouldn't do that, (would you?)

....

Adjectives and their opposites

2 Write the opposites to these adjectives. In pairs, discuss which can be applied to people, which to a job and which to a written report. (Some words apply to more than one category.)

e.g. interesting ......*uninteresting*......................

a efficient ....

b reliable ....

c dishonest ....

d generous ....

e intolerant ....

f pleasant ....

g intelligent ....

h thoughtless ....

i polite ....

j hard working ....

k organised ....

l quiet ....

Appearance and dress

3 Look at the photograph of Nuria Baffuto. Mark the notes true ☐T☐, false ☐F☐ or don't know ☐?☐. What else would you say about Nuria? How would you describe Atsuo Sato?

Nuria Baffuto

Atsuo Sato

Nuria Baffuto

quite tall, slim ☐   a silk blouse ☐

has straight blond hair ☐   flat shoes ☐

is wearing a trouser suit ☐

Recommendations and suggestions

4 Note these common phrases.

Can/Could I make a suggestion?

Why don't you …?

I don't think you should … You shouldn't …
It's not a good idea to …

Work in pairs.

Partner A: You are Nuria or Atsuo.

Partner B: Suggest which clothes they might wear …

a … for reorganising a storeroom.

b … for taking clients to a formal dinner.

c … for a trip to the coast.

e.g. I don't think you should wear a suit. Why don't you wear some overalls?

4 | Listening

Talking about your job

Listen to Sonya Reed talking about what it is like to work for a manufacturing company based in the south of England. Then answer the questions.

a What is her present job?
b What does the job involve?
c When does she have dealings with the factory floor?
d How does she feel about her lack of contact with the shop floor?
e How long has she been with the company?
f Has she always had the same job?
g What does she do in her free time?
h Would you like to swap lifestyles/jobs with Sonya. Why? Why not?

5 | Application

A brief job history

1 Read the article about Tim Berners-Lee, the founder of the Internet. Use a dictionary to check any words which prevent you from understanding the text.

2 Referring to the article and to other language presented and practised in this unit, write your own brief job history.

CHILD OF THE COMPUTER AGE

Tim Berners-Lee grew up in the London of the Swinging Sixties, the child of computer programmer parents who worked on the first commercial computer, the Ferranti Mark I. Not surprisingly, perhaps, his childhood featured making computers out of cardboard and playing games with imaginary numbers. Later, studying physics at Oxford, he progressed to building a working computer using an old TV, a Motorola microprocessor and a soldering iron (he was banned from using the university's computer when he and a friend were caught hacking).

On graduating, Tim worked as a programmer in the UK and in Switzerland, at the particle physics institute CERN, where he developed the World Wide Web – the system for organising, linking and browsing information on the Internet that we all use today. For the World Wide Web, Berners-Lee devised HTML (hypertext mark-up language), the URL (universal resource locator) address system, and the HTTP (hypertext transfer) protocol that allows documents to be linked to each other.

As early as 1991, he offered the World Wide Web on the Internet for free. He has never sought to cash in on his invention. 'The web exploded because it was free,' he says. 'If I had kept control of it, it would never have taken off.' In 1993, in order to safeguard the future of the web, he founded the World Wide Web Consortium, also known as W3C, at the Massachusetts Institute of Technology (MIT). Tim Berners-Lee was knighted recently in recognition of his far-reaching technological contributions.

Adapted from the *Holland Herald* – KLM, online

LANGUAGE REFERENCE

Language notes

For more detailed notes, see the Business Grammar Guide.

Replying to negative statements

Note the following examples.

You don't agree with me.
To confirm: No, I don't.
To deny: Yes, I do.

She didn't phone.
To confirm: No, she didn't.
To deny: Yes, she did.

They didn't give you the job.
To confirm: No, they didn't.
To deny: Yes, they did.

This isn't your signature.
To confirm: No, it isn't.
To deny: Yes, it is.

Some adjectives to describe appearance and dress

Some common materials:
cotton, leather, silk, wool, denim, corduroy, nylon, acrylic, lycra, polyester

Some common designs:
floral, plain, spotted, striped, checked

Some adjectives describing colours:
bright, dark, light, pastel, pale

Some adjectives describing hair:
blond, fair, grey, dark, curly, wavy, straight, short, thinning

Forming the opposites of adjectives

un- is the most common negative prefix.
e.g. profitable/unprofitable
       safe/unsafe

in- is another common negative prefix. It becomes *im-* before an *m* or *p*; *ir-* before an *r*; and *il-* before an *l*.
e.g. direct/indirect
       flexible/inflexible
       possible/impossible
       mobile/immobile
       legal/illegal
       relevant/irrelevant

dis- is another common negative prefix.
e.g. honest/dishonest
       organised/disorganised
       encouraging/discouraging (not *disencouraging*)

-less is a common negative suffix.
e.g. colourful/colourless

Useful phrases

Kasha Meld is a qualified accountant.
She joined the company last year.
She trained as an accountant with Touche Ross.
Sanjay Patel studied law at university.
He also has a degree in business studies.

Maurice Pot is responsible for the day-to-day running of the department.
He has to liaise with the production manager.
He spends a lot of his time advising people.
He doesn't have much to do with the sales side of the business.

What's Kasha like?
She's honest and reliable.
       dishonest   unreliable
She's experienced and efficient.
       inexperienced   inefficient

What does Maurice look like?
He's quite tall. He has curly dark hair.
What's he wearing today?
He's wearing a pin-striped suit and a yellow spotted tie.
Kasha's wearing a light-coloured trouser suit.

Do you think I should wear a jacket and tie?
I don't need to wear a tie, do I?
No, you don't. It's a very informal occasion.
I need to wear something smart, don't I?
Yes, you do. It's going to be a formal dinner.

UNIT 10 Buying products

1 Overview

Key dialogues

Listen to the dialogues and answer the questions.

a Which model of clock is the caller interested in?
What is the nearest equivalent like?

b Are the crates available in all sizes?
How long does delivery take?

c What were the features of the 'classic' watch?
Why is the customer disappointed?

d Which trampolines did they use to make?
What are the dimensions of the 'Funster' trampoline?

> **Preparation**
>
> Bring to the lesson price lists, brochures or product descriptions. These can refer to any products which you are interested in.
>
> Be prepared to ask and answer questions about products, based on the price lists, etc. Talk about prices, serial/reference numbers, materials (*What is it made of?*) and dimensions (*What size is it?*, *What does it weigh?*, etc.)
>
> Look at the unit Language Reference on page 52.

2 Practice

Ordering products

Work in pairs.

Partner A: Your information is below. You wish to order 20 of each of these wall clocks, but you only have an old copy of a brochure.

Partner B: Your information is on page 134, and comes from the up-to-date website.

> **Useful language**
>
> I would like to order …
> Do you still stock …?
> You used to supply …
> What is the nearest equivalent?
> What are the dimensions?
> What are its key features?

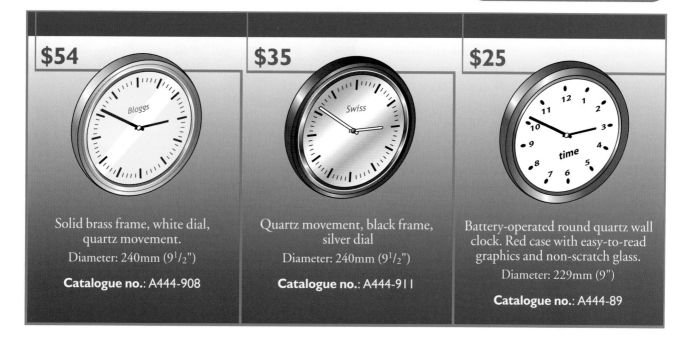

$54
Solid brass frame, white dial, quartz movement.
Diameter: 240mm (9$^1/_2$")
Catalogue no.: A444-908

$35
Quartz movement, black frame, silver dial
Diameter: 240mm (9$^1/_2$")
Catalogue no.: A444-911

$25
Battery-operated round quartz wall clock. Red case with easy-to-read graphics and non-scratch glass.
Diameter: 229mm (9")
Catalogue no.: A444-89

3 Language focus

Check the Language Notes on page 52 as you do these exercises.

Numbers and symbols

1 Write out the numbers, letters and symbols.

e.g. 104T/2-55A *one oh four T slash two hyphen five five A*

a 12/4734-AZ97   **e** 14 sq m

b 17-VLD/44/900   **f** 37 cu cm

c $^3/_8$ **g** 25% = $^1/_4$

d $^1/_{10}$ **h** 66.6% = $^2/_3$

Materials and substances

2 Name two materials or substances that might be used in the production of the following items.

a a desk   ....

b a keyboard ....

c a bridge   ....

d a wall   ....

e a suit   ....

f a suitcase   ....

g a violin   ....

h a sandwich ....

used to

3 Write five statements about products/services you used to/didn't use to buy or use and/or things you used to/didn't used to do. Compare your statements with other members of your group.

e.g. *I used to print out my messages, but now my office is completely paperless! We didn't use to spend so much on courier services.*

4 Listening

Key selling points

1 Match the products with the key selling points.

a Industrial clothing   **i** Stylish and very economical

b Educational toys   **ii** Highly competitive prices and very durable

c Furniture and fittings   **iii** Quality, price, original designs

d Glass conservatories   **iv** Extremely well made, three-month guarantee

2 Describe some of the products you buy regularly. Why do you buy them? Use adverbs such as *highly competitive* and *reasonably priced* in your statements.

e.g. I buy suits from Ato Clothing. They are always beautifully made and very stylish.

3 Write an email in which you recommend a particular product. Describe the points which support your recommendation.

5 | Application

Making a product enquiry

1 Read the exchange of letters. Then answer the questions below.

SM Electrics

67 Dune Heights, Woollamoora, NSW Australia
Tel: 39 41 521   Fax: 39 42 670

The Sales Manager
RA Plastics
56 Marino Road
Singapore 0923
Republic of Singapore

Ref 12/AS/DB
1 June 2…

Dear Sir/Madam

We are a major manufacturer of electrical goods for the Australian market, and we are currently reviewing our list of suppliers of components. Your company has been recommended to us by R. G. Holdsworth as a reliable producer of plastic casing.

We would be very grateful if you could forward details of your range of products, together with price lists and delivery charges.

We look forward to hearing from you by 20 June, at which time we shall be finalising our plans to visit prospective suppliers in the ASEAN area.

Yours faithfully

Andrea P. Soleman

Andrea Soleman
Chief Buyer

RA PLASTICS

56 Marino Road, Singapore 0923
Republic of Singapore
Tel: 33 64 119   Fax: 33 64 129

Your ref: 12/AS/DB
14 June 2…

Ms Andrea Soleman
SM Electrics
67 Dune Heights
Woollamoora, NSW
Australia

Dear Ms Soleman

Thank you for your letter of 1 June. I enclose details of our product range, price lists and delivery terms, as requested.

We were extremely interested in your enquiry and we very much hope that you will be able to visit us in Singapore. I am sure that there are many areas in which we can cooperate.

Please contact us as soon as you know your itinerary.

Yours sincerely

Tony Pang Wan

Tony Pang Wan
Sales Manager

---

a What is SM Electrics' main market?
b Who recommended RA Plastics?
c What information does Andrea Soleman need?
d Why does she need it by 20 June?
e What is Tony Pang Wan's response to the enquiry?

2 Work in pairs. Follow the sequence below. Refer to the brochures, price lists, etc. which you have brought to class.

Partner A: Write a product enquiry to **Partner B**.
Partner B: Reply to **Partner A**'s letter.
Partner A: Call **Partner B** to discuss details.
Partners A and B: Write emails to confirm points covered in the phone call.

LANGUAGE REFERENCE

Language notes

For more detailed notes, see the Business Grammar Guide.

Adverbs in phrases

We can use adverbs to modify adjectives.

e.g. **absolutely accurate, really expensive, completely reliable**

We can use adverbs to modify past participles.

e.g. **extremely well-made, highly recommended, beautifully designed**

Numbers and symbols

Reference numbers:

106/B-2	one oh six stroke B dash two
A3/077-PP	A three slash zero seven seven hyphen double P (or PP)

Dimensions:

10m × 6.5m	ten by six point five metres
10m × 10m	ten metres square
10m^2	ten square metres
10m^3	ten cubic metres

Fractions:

$^2/_3$	two-thirds
$^3/_4$	three-quarters
$^1/_{12}$	a/one-twelfth
$^3/_8 = 37.5\%$	three-eighths equals thirty-seven point five per cent

Some materials and metals

Some common metals:

aluminium, chrome, copper, iron, steel, brass, silver, gold, zinc

Other common materials:

concrete, brick, glass, plastic, stone, wood, quartz, rubber, cardboard, polystyrene, fibreglass, leather

Used to

Affirmative:

You used to stock wall clocks.
They used to be our best line.

Negative:

We didn't (did not) use to advertise.
Nobody used to buy them.

Interrogative:

Where did you use to get them?
Did they use to sell well?
Did we use to supply many?

Short answers:

Yes, they did.   No, they didn't.
Yes, we did.   No, we didn't.

Examples:

I used to work in Australia.
That line didn't use to be very popular.
We never used to get any complaints.
Did you use to make them in a larger size?

Useful phrases

Our products are reasonably priced.

competitively priced   conveniently packaged
extremely well made   highly competitive

What are they made of?
The casing is made of plastic.
The working parts are all stainless steel.
The components are made in Spain.

The base is made of concrete.
Twenty-five per cent of the components are rubber.
Two-thirds of the parts are made of copper.
The structure covers an area of 5 square metres.

We stock the full product range.
Most items are available from stock.
The XC range is currently out of stock.
When can you deliver the goods?
We offer next-day delivery.
Delivery usually takes two days.

How much do they cost?
How much are they?

The reference number is 12/473-AZ9.
I'd like to order one.
Do you still supply them in green?
I'm afraid we don't stock that colour anymore.
That line is discontinued.

We used to make them in that size.
We used to stock that design.
It used to be very popular, but there's no longer any demand for it.
What is the nearest equivalent?
The A444-909 is very similar.

UNIT 11 Product descriptions

Preparation

The focus of this unit is on how products are made, so bring to the lesson any technical literature, sales literature or specifications for products which interest you.

This unit also builds on Unit 10, so you can refer back to your preparation materials for that unit.

Refer to the Useful Phrases and Language Notes for this unit, which are on page 56.

1 Overview

Key dialogues

Listen to the exchanges and answer the questions.

a In which area does the company specialise?
  Are their products always made to order?
b How much experience does the customer's child have?
  Why is the range suitable for children?
c How is the groundsheet of the tent attached to the upper section?
  What are the fibre-optic rods for?

2 Practice

Checking product information

Cameron Balloons is the world's largest manufacturer of hot air balloons. Read the information about its 'O-type' envelope and mark these statements true [T], false [F] or don't know [?].

a The O-type envelope is cheaper than the N-type. ☐
b The O-type is a very versatile balloon. ☐
c The use of Hyperlast fabric is standard. ☐
d All balloon baskets can be made to suit the customer. ☐
e All Cameron balloons come with a lifetime guarantee. ☐

The 'O-type' envelope

The slightly bulbous 12 gore O-type envelope (balloon) offers a cost advantage against equivalent sizes in our top-of-the-market Cameron N-type range and superior artwork display opportunities when compared with the lower-cost Viva.

The O-type is ideally suited to fun flying, promotional work or passenger carrying. Envelope variants from 31,000 to 160,000ft^3 (890 to 4530m^3) in size cater for the pilot who dangles his feet from a one-person air-chair to the pilot who wants to fly up to nine people.

Exclusive tartan weave fabric – resistant to fungal attack and fading – is standard while Hyperlast, the long-life balloon fabric that is silicone coated on both sides, is optional.

There is a wide range of baskets, all of which can be customised with coloured banding and your choice of suede or leather trim. Single, double and triple burners are available in various combinations. And there's one very special no-cost accessory we supply with every balloon: a written guarantee of Cameron quality.

From: www.cameronballoons.com

Refer to the Language Notes on page 56 as you complete these exercises.

Present Perfect Continuous tense

1 Put one verb in the Present Perfect Simple and the other in the continuous.

a He .... (never meet) the MD.
He .... (work) for the company for 11 years.

b They .... (make) hang-gliders since 1998.
They .... (produce) over 3000 hang-gliders in that time.

c I .... (call) clients all morning.
I .... (only speak) to five so far.

d It .... (rain) three times this week.
It .... (rain) all day today.

Indirect questions

2 Write an indirect form of these questions, using *Do you know …?, I'd like to know …, Can you tell me …?*, etc.

e.g. What does it look like?
    Can you tell me what it looks like?

a How big is it?
....

b Does it run on petrol or gas?
....

c How often does it need servicing?
....

d Where can I buy it?
....

e Can you deliver it on Friday afternoon?
....

f How soon can you arrange delivery?
....

The Present Simple Passive tense

3 Listen to someone describing how a balloon is made. Put these steps in the right order. Notice how the Simple Present Passive tense (*it is made, The panels are sewn*, etc.) is used to describe a process.

a Holes are made in the 'envelope'. ☐

b The nylon is cut into panels. ☐

c Wires are used to connect the envelope with the burner. ☐

d The nylon panels are sewn together. ☐

4 Describe a production process which you are familiar with. Then write a description of the process. Refer to the audioscript and notes on the Simple Present Passive to help you.

Shapes

5 Match the shapes and the objects. Describe other familiar objects.

a	round	**i**	an American football
b	square	**ii**	a plus sign
c	oval	**iii**	a pyramid
d	triangular	**iv**	a wheel
e	rectangular	**v**	a chess board
f	heart-shaped	**vi**	a golf club
g	L-shaped	**vii**	a shield
h	in the shape of a cross	**viii**	a football pitch

Promotional gifts

1 Read the descriptions of promotional recycled products, then answer the questions.
Use a dictionary where necessary.

a Which is the most expensive product advertised?
b Which is the cheapest?
c Which other product mentioned is made from recyclable material?
d Which is the largest product advertised?
e Which is the smallest?

f How many products are made from recycled vending cups?
g How many products are made of wood?
h Which item, in your view, is the best value?
i Which other products would choose to promote your own products?

RECYCLED PRODUCTS

Need recycled products to match your promotion?

Here is a selection of what we can offer. Apart from the items shown, all our plastic carrier bags are made from recyclable material and all our paper products are available from recycled paper at a small extra cost (prices on application).

Recycled ballpens

Made from recycled computer printers. Price includes 1 colour print in area 45×20mm.

1000 @ 28p each.
5000 @ 23p each.

MORE INFORMATION AND TO ORDER

Recycled pencils

Made from 1 recycled vending cup. Price includes 1 colour print in area 60×20mm.
1000 @ 23p each.
5000 @ 20p each.

MORE INFORMATION AND TO ORDER

Rulers 12"

Made from recycled vending cups. Price includes 1 colour print in area 220×15mm (30cm).
1000 @ 38p each. 5000 @ 32p each.

MORE INFORMATION AND TO ORDER

Rulers 6"

Made from recycled vending cups. Price includes 1 colour print in area 100×15mm (15cm).
1000 @ 29p each. 5000 @ 27p each.

MORE INFORMATION AND TO ORDER

Describing products

Revise the language presented in this unit. Then prepare a short presentation, describing the following.

a Your product range, or one which you are familiar with.
b A particular product.
c The special features of the product.
d How the product is made.

From eamcadgifts

LANGUAGE REFERENCE

Language notes

For more detailed notes, see the Business Grammar Guide.

The Present Perfect Continuous tense

Affirmative:

I've (I have) been waiting for an hour.

It's (It has) been raining since this morning.

Negative:

They haven't (have not) been listening.

It hasn't (has not) been selling well.

Interrogative:

What have you been doing all morning?

Has he been talking about this for long?

Have you been travelling since yesterday?

Short answers:

Yes, he has.   No, he hasn't.

Yes, we have.   No, we haven't

Examples:

How long have you been producing this line?

We've been marketing this product since 2003.

Indirect questions

Note the following examples of questions.

e.g. Can/could you tell me if you have it in stock?

Do you know when they'll be ready?

I'd like to know how much it is.

Note the following examples of responses to indirect questions.

e.g. I don't know whether we have them in stock.

I'll have to check how much it is.

The Present Simple Passive tense

Affirmative:

I'm (I am) employed by …

The two sheets are stapled together.

Negative:

Normally, he isn't (is not) consulted.

We aren't (are not) contacted until …

Interrogative:

Is it manufactured locally?

Are they sewn together?

Short answers:

Yes, it is.   No, it isn't.

Yes, they are.   No, they aren't.

Examples:

Are you invited to those meetings?

It isn't handled by this department.

The sections are painted by hand.

Useful phrases

How long have you been making balloons?

For just over 20 years.

What about the 'P' series?

We've only been selling that model since the beginning of this year.

We're the largest manufacturer of balloons in the world.

On average, we build one every day.

No other manufacturer can match our experience.

These balloons are particularly suitable for beginners.

They range in size from 590 cubic metres to 2550 cubic metres.

That's 90,000 cubic feet.

We also sell off-the-shelf packages.

All are available at the lowest possible prices.

They come in a range of colours and sizes.

There are various options.

Which different shapes are available?

Do you have any round ones?

This one is L-shaped.

That one is in the shape of a cross.

This is how they are made.

First, the fabric is cut into panels.

Then the panels are sewn together.

At this stage, the structure is reinforced.

Finally, it's connected to the frame.

Could you tell me if this is the latest version of the software?

Do you know whether it runs on this type of PC?

I'd like to know how often it needs updating.

UNIT 12 Faults and breakdowns

1 Overview

Key dialogues

Listen and answer the questions.

a What is the caller complaining about?
How can the supplier put things right?

b Why is the customer happy?
Does the caller need anything else?

c What is 'the list of complaints'?
Who is employed to deal with complaints?

d What is the feedback from the customer?
Why was the speaker surprised?

Preparation

Bring to the lesson some emails and letters of complaint and/or letters in which you have complimented suppliers for good products and service.

What do you, typically, have to complain about or chase up? Late delivery, perhaps, or faulty goods? Be prepared to describe the levels of customer service that you received.

Refer to the unit Language Notes and Useful Phrases on page 60.

2 Practice

Satisfaction and dissatisfaction

1 Note these examples of compliments and responses. Work in pairs. **Partner A** praises a product that he/she has bought. **Partner B** responds.

Compliments

We were/have been very pleased with it.
It was/has been excellent.
It worked/has been working very well indeed.
We have not had any trouble with it since we've had it/since we bought it.

Responses

Yes, we are very pleased with it too.
We have had excellent feedback from our customers.
We have had a good response from our clients.
That's good to hear.
Thank you for telling us.

2 Note these examples of complaints and responses. Work in pairs. **Partner A** complains about **Partner B**'s product. **Partner B** responds.

Complaints

We'd/I'd like to make a complaint.
We are very unhappy about …
[Its performance] isn't good enough.
[The noise it makes] is terrible.
It has broken down [three times] since we bought it.

Responses

What exactly is the problem?
We are very sorry (about it).
That is very unfortunate.
I am very sorry to hear that.
What can we do to put it right?

3 Language focus

Check the Language Notes on page 60 as you do these exercises.

Relative pronouns

1 Rewrite the examples using *who, which, whose, where* etc.

e.g. This is the woman. Her car was damaged.
This is the woman whose car was damaged.

a The hotel was expensive. I stayed there.

....

b I wrote down the number. He gave it to me.

....

c Have you found that file? You lost it yesterday.

....

d I drove to Leoton. We have an good customer there.

....

e The man is very helpful. He works in the office next to mine.

....

f I work for a Taiwanese company. It specialises in customer care.

....

g That's the man. It's his job to deal with these enquiries.

....

Order of adjectives

2 Use adjectives from the box to describe the products below. Then write descriptions of your own products/products that you use.

▶ shiny	▶ copy	▶ HP	▶ smoke
▶ fibreglass	▶ plastic	▶ nylon	▶ stainless steel
▶ French	▶ Swedish	▶ Japanese	▶ American
▶ Italian	▶ green	▶ black	▶ grey
▶ blue	▶ cream	▶ square	▶ new
▶ cheap	▶ faulty	▶ efficient	▶ light

e.g. hockey stick *a black fibreglass hockey stick*

a phone ....

b alarm ....

c machine..

d desk..

e printer..

need + -ing

3 Listen to the conversation between a garage owner and a person who is considering buying the car. What is wrong with the car? Choose from the words and phrases in the box.

▶ scratched	▶ broken	▶ dented
▶ doesn't work	▶ loose	▶ bent
▶ leaking	▶ stiff	▶ cracked

a paintwork ....

b bumper ....

c petrol tank ....

d headlamps ....

e windows..

f petrol gauge ....

4 Write other sentences using *need*. Think of things in your life that need doing or buying.

e.g. *I need a new laptop.*
My laptop needs replacing.
We need new fans.
The old fans need replacing.
I need new strings on my tennis racquet.
My racquet needs restringing.

....

....

....

....

A faulty product

1 Read the product recall notice. Then mark the statements below true ⊤, false ⊥ or don't know ?. Why has the notice been issued?

   a All XC-4 models are faulty. ☐
   b The XC-4 can be clearly identified. ☐
   c The code number is visible on the front. ☐
   d The cost of testing the faulty models will be high. ☐
   e The notice has been issued because

   ....

2 Work in pairs.
   Partner A: You work for PX Alarms.
   Partner B: You are a customer.
   Partner A calls **Partner B** to inform him/her about the fault with the XC-4 range.

   ┌───┐
   │ **Some useful language**   │
   │ How can I identify the faulty alarms?   │
   │ Are the other alarms in your range affected? │
   │ Will you collect the faulty alarms?, etc.│
   └───┘

IMPORTANT SAFETY NOTICE:

Smoke Alarms

As a responsible company, PX Alarms, a division of the PX group of companies, is recalling all of its XC-4 range of smoke alarms.

We have discovered a fault which may invalidate the working of a number of the alarms in this range.

To identify the alarm, please remove from the wall and check the code on the back of the casing; the code is clearly stamped on the back. Only the range coded XC-4 is affected. All other alarms are completely unaffected.

If you have an XC-4 alarm, please stop using it immediately and return it to us at the address below for testing. All postage and testing costs will be borne by PX Alarms.

The company would like to apologise for any inconvenience caused.

LANGUAGE REFERENCE

Language notes

For more detailed notes, see the Business Grammar Guide.

Some notes on relative pronouns

Note when we use *who* or *that*.

e.g. the engineers who/that serviced it
the woman who/that made the complaint

Note when we use *which* or *that*.

e.g. a product which/that sells well
a company which/that makes pharmaceuticals

Note when we can omit *who/which/that*.

e.g. the salesman (who/that) I spoke to
the advertisement (which/that) I saw

Note when we use *where*.

e.g. the town where the factory is
the office where I work

Note when we use *whose*.

e.g. employees whose work is satisfactory
a firm whose main market is Korea

The order of adjectives

Note the following examples.

e.g. a large, red container
a small, rectangular table
a white, polystyrene box
a beautiful long, Kirghiz jacket
black, leather golfing shoes
a faulty, plastic smoke alarm
a new, fibreglass tennis racquet

Useful phrases

I would like to return …
… some faulty, plastic smoke alarms.
… this lightweight graphite tennis racquet.
Some parts need replacing.
It needs sorting out.

The windows don't close properly.
The control system doesn't work.
There is something wrong with the case.
It's scratched.

| broken | dented | cracked |
| faulty | damaged | substandard |

We're very unhappy about the quality.
It isn't good enough.
I'm sorry to hear that.
We're very sorry.
We apologise for any inconvenience.
What can we do to put it right?

I spoke to the man who wrote the report.
I contacted the customer who made the complaint.
I'll phone the person whose job it is to mend it.

The customer was very pleased with the replacement.
He says it's been working very well indeed.
He hasn't had any more trouble with it.

That's good to hear.
Thank you for saying that.
I appreciate that.

UNIT 13 The services you provide and use

Preparation

Bring to the class brochures or notes about services you provide or use.

Prepare to introduce the information which you bring to class. Also prepare to identify other services which you are offered in your daily life, e.g. staff training, tax advice, computer consultancy, food delivery, window cleaning, etc.

Refer to the Language Notes and Useful Phrases for this unit on page 64.

1 Overview

Key dialogues

Listen and answer the questions.

a What does the service contract include?
  How is it good value for money?
b Do they handle their own security?
  Why do they subcontract services like transport?
c What is the cost of leasing?
  What is the cost of outright purchase?
d What is the list price of the equipment?
  What is the offer price?

2 Practice

The services you use

Complete the table by listing services which you use, providers of services and your reasons for using them. What do you look for? Compare your lists and comments with a partner.

Service	Provider(s)	Reason for choice	Other comments
e.g. Security	VU-Secure	Friendly staff. Competitive prices. Highly professional.	The company mainly employs former police officers.

3 | Listening

Talking about services

Listen and match speakers a–d with the services provided. Is the service described one they provide ☐P☐ or one they use ☐U☐? Underline the reason for use.

Service	Speaker (a–d)	P/U	Reason for use
express parcel delivery	d		speed / insurance cover
emergency breakdown		P	good reputation / short waiting time
site maintenance			the cheapest option / a time-saving strategy
crèche			friendly staff / <u>good value</u>

4 | Language focus

Check the Language Notes on page 64 as you do these exercises.

to have/get something done

1 Respond to the statements, using the verbs in the box.

> ▶ update   ▶ replace   ▶ service   ▶ paint
> ▶ repair   ▶ clean ✓   ▶ change

e.g. The office carpet is very dirty.

(need) *We need to have it cleaned.*

a We've got some graffiti on the walls.
(must) ....

b One of the machines has broken down.
(have to) ....

c My car tyres are worn out.
(need) ....

d Our accounting system is very old-fashioned.
(ought to) ....

e My phone battery is losing its charge.
(must) ....

f We are having some problems with our printer.
(should) ....

Reflexive pronouns and *myself, my own*

2 In pairs, discuss which of these jobs you do yourselves, and which you have done for you?

e.g. I clean my flat myself.
I have my office cleaned for me.
I make my own flight arrangements.

> ▶ photocopying
> ▶ making coffee
> ▶ office cleaning
> ▶ posting letters
> ▶ ordering taxis
> ▶ car maintenance
> ▶ booking flights
> ▶ redecorating house/flat
> ▶ gardening
> ▶ cleaning the drains

Lease or purchase

1 Read the arguments, which set out the advantages and disadvantages of leasing. Refer to the glossary (page 158) and to a dictionary to check any unfamiliar words.

2 As a group, decide on a common business environment. Then decide whether or not to buy or lease some office equipment. Write down the reasons for your decision.

Copiers: leasing vs. buying

To lease a copier or not to lease a copier? Everyone's circumstances are different, but photocopier leasing is very popular and most OER Group customers generally decide that leasing is right for their business. That said, contact your financial adviser to discuss how best to acquire equipment. In the meantime, though, please consider some advantages and disadvantages of leasing your copier.

Advantages of leasing a copier

1 Costs for the copier are certain and are known in advance.

2 The copier cannot be withdrawn once the contract is signed and its conditions complied with.

3 There's no need to tie up capital in fixed assets such as copiers.

4 Allowances, depreciation and other calculations are not needed, since leasing is concerned only with rentals.

5 Leasing provides a medium-term source of capital which may not be available elsewhere.

6 Leasing provides a hedge against inflation, as the use of the asset is obtained immediately; payments are made out of future funds and are made in fixed money terms, with real costs falling as inflation increases.

Disadvantages of leasing a copier

1 It is generally not possible to dispose of the copier before the end of the lease.

2 The copier is not owned.

3 Funds must be found to pay the lease throughout its duration.

Should you decide to lease a copier, then OER Group provides extremely competitive leasing rates from major lenders.

LANGUAGE REFERENCE

Language notes

For more detailed notes, see the Business Grammar Guide.

Rentals and charges

Note the following examples.

e.g. The rental is €9.50 a day.
It has to be paid monthly.
We are invoiced quarterly.
They charge a €1000 per quarter.
She earns $50,000 per year.
The service charge is reviewed every six months.

Note the following abbreviations.

pa = *per annum* (Latin), per year, annually
pd = per day, daily
pw = per week, weekly

to have/get something done

have/get + noun + past participle is used when we get someone else to do something for us.

e.g. We only **had** the copier **serviced** two weeks ago.

It is often used after modal verbs.

e.g. We **need to get** the printer **repaired**.
We **must have** the windows **cleaned**.
We **should get** some photographs **taken**.
We **ought to have** the system **updated**.
Where can I **get** this machine **serviced**?
Where can I **have** my suit **cleaned**?

myself, ourselves, my own, etc.

myself	ourselves
yourself	yourselves
himself/herself/itself	themselves
my own	our own
your own	your own
his/her/its own	their own

Note how we use these to emphasise who does something.

e.g. I make all **my** travel arrangements **myself**.
I make all **my own** travel arrangements.

We do **our** repairs **ourselves**.
We do **our own** repairs.
Do you have to do the work **yourself/selves**?

We also use *myself*, etc. when the subject and the object of a sentence are the same.

e.g. **I** burnt **myself** yesterday. (not *I burnt me*)
Could **you** introduce **yourselves**?

Useful phrases

We do the office cleaning ourselves.
We handle our own cleaning.
We manage everything in-house.
We subcontract our logistics to CLK.
Routine maintenance work is done by an outside contractor.

CLK provides an excellent service.
The service they provide is very good value.

We ought to have our IT system updated.
We need to have all of our machines serviced.
We must get the job done soon.

We're considering whether to lease or to buy.
What's the cost of outright purchase?
What does it cost to lease?

There's a discount of 20% if you buy today.
There's a 20% discount.
The net price is $1512.
Sales tax is extra.

The rental is €95 per day.

per week	weekly
per month	monthly

We offer a full service contract.
What does the contract include?
It covers routine and emergency call-outs.
It doesn't cover spare parts.
The service charge is $690 per annum.
The first six months are free of charge.

UNIT 14 Service issues

1 Overview

Key dialogues

Listen to the conversations and answer the questions.

a When did the first speaker expect to have received payment?
What does the second speaker promise to do?

b When was delivery promised?
What has happened to it?

c Why have they cancelled the course?
What does the organiser offer?

d What is the problem?
What's the good news?

Preparation

Bring to the class correspondence or documents relating to service issues. If you have no examples written in English, you may like to translate any which you have in your own language.

Prepare to talk through the documents which you bring to class.

Refer to the Language Reference section for this unit on page 68.

2 Practice

Dealing with service issues

Working in pairs, practise dealing with some service issues, such as a printer breakdown, the late delivery of a package, the non-arrival of consultant, etc. There are some examples of apologies in the Language Notes on page 68.

Partner A: Query/complain. Accept or reject **Partner B**'s apologies. Accept or reject **Partner B**'s proposed solutions.

Partner B: Offer explanations. Express regret. Propose alternatives or solutions.

You guaranteed a 24-hour call-out service. We've been waiting for your engineer for two days.

You said that the money would be transferred by the end of the week. It still hasn't arrived. Could you check what has happened?

You promised us next-day delivery. That was two days ago.

You should have let us know immediately. You obviously knew that your stocks were running low. We have had to stop one of our machines because of this.

We are very sorry about this. I'll arrange for immediate delivery. I'll find out what has happened and call you back.

3 Language focus

Check the Language Notes on page 68 as you do these exercises.

The Past tense of modal verbs

1 Respond to the statements.
e.g. Why didn't you tell us?
(I should/tell/you)
I should have told you. I'm sorry.

a Where did you leave your papers?
(I/must/leave/them/in the office)

b Your line was engaged all day.
(you/could/send/me/a text message)

c Why did you book me into that hotel?
(you /should/check with me/first)

d Why did you need to call Linda?
(she/might/forget/about/the meeting)

e We were disappointed with the way they handled it.
(they/ought to/let us know)

f We have plenty of items in stock.
(we/need not/reordered/yet)

g There was no need to send a car for him.
(he/could/walk)

h The call-out engineer made a mess of the repairs.
(we/should/do/the job/ourselves)

Apologising and accepting/rejecting apologies

2 Match the apologies with the responses in the box below.

a Sorry I'm so late. The traffic was terrible coming out of the airport. □

b Sorry, I don't follow you. □

c I do apologise for all the trouble we've caused. □

d Excuse me, do you mind if I interrupt for a moment? □

e I'd like to apologise for not coming to yesterday's meeting. □

i	Of course not. Go ahead.
ii	Yes, it's a shame you couldn't come. You could have let us know.
iii	Let me put it another way then.
iv	You should have called us from the airport. We were getting worried about you.
v	Don't worry. It's been no trouble. It really doesn't matter.

3 Practise making apologies and accepting them. Think of some situations when you need to apologise.

e.g. You cannot deliver goods because of a strike. You are going to be late for a meeting, etc.

4 Listening

A delivery problem

Listen to a conversation about a consignment which has failed to arrive. Then answer the questions.

a Which service did the customer use?
b What is the parcel reference number?
c When will Ernst Capel call back?
d What is the driver's story?
e What is Tara Vene's main concern?
f What action is she going to take?

Customer service

1 Study the letter from Faith Vere and the reply from Rachel Dill. In pairs, discuss the tone of the letters. Are your sympathies with Leaders Training or with Melto?

64 place d'Orsel, 93002 Paris
Tel: (1) 42 27 33688
Fax: (1) 42 27 37190

25 February 2...

Dear Ms Dill

Leadership and Motivation Course, 2–3 March

We regret that we have had to cancel this course due to an insufficient number of enrolments. The next Leadership and Motivation Course will be held on 2–3 June, and I have enrolled Mr Forest and Ms Lomo for these dates.

We apologise for any inconvenience which this might cause.

Yours sincerely

Faith C. Vere

Faith Vere
Bookings Administrator

97 Belgrave Crescent, Aberdeen 40C 9GL, Scotland
Tel: 02761 309427; Fax: 02761 896 438

28 February 2...

Dear Ms Vere

Leadership and Motivation Course, 2–3 March

I was very surprised to receive your letter of 25 February and, I must admit, rather annoyed. You should have let us know sooner if you were planning to cancel the course. There was no indication in your course publicity that a course would be cancelled if there were not enough applicants. This fact should have been made clear in your advertising material.

I am also very unhappy about the way you have assumed that Mr Forest and Ms Lomo will attend your June course. In fact, these dates are not suitable for them.

I therefore ask you to cancel their places on this course and to refund the deposit which we have paid. I believe you have the number of our bank account.

Yours sincerely

R. Dill

Rachel Dill
Group Training Coordinator
Melto Ltd

2 In pairs, **Partner A** (Faith Vere) phones **Partner B** (Rachel Dill) to smooth over the situation, e.g.
I was sorry to hear that you wish to cancel ...
I understand that ...
I was unhappy about ...
Are there other suitable dates?, etc.

LANGUAGE REFERENCE

Language notes

For more detailed notes, see the Business Grammar Guide.

The past tense of modal verbs

The modal verbs are *can*, *could*, *may*, *might*, *must*, *ought to*, *have to*, *shall*, *should*, *will* and *would*.

Affirmative:

He must have forgotten.
They may have left already.

Negative:

He won't (will not) have gone yet.
I shouldn't (should not) have mentioned it.

Interrogative:

Who can have called?
Would you have accepted …?
Might he have done it?

Short answers:

Yes, I would.   No, I wouldn't.
Yes, he might.   No, he wouldn't.

Note: The short answer *No, he mightn't* is not possible.

Examples:

The delivery should have arrived by now.
You ought to have made the situation clear.
You could have sent me a text message.
He may have lost the address.
We apologise for any inconvenience this might have caused you.

Some examples of apologies

Making apologies:

I'm very sorry to have to interrupt you, but …
I'm sorry (that) I didn't call earlier.
We'd like to apologise for not finishing on time.
We do apologise for any problems this might cause you.
Please accept our apologies.

Accepting apologies:

That's OK. / Not at all. / Don't worry.
It's no problem. / Never mind.
It really doesn't matter.
Please don't apologise.
There's (really) no need to apologise.

Rejecting apologies:

You should have let us know.
You ought to have made the situation clear.
I'm sorry, but I'm not happy about this.
Please make sure that it doesn't happen again.
(Take care with using these strong rejections of apologies.)

Useful phrases

We regret that we've had to cancel the course due to insufficient demand.
… because of financial difficulties.
… as a result of complaints by customers.

We've just heard that the delivery hasn't arrived.
As far as I know, they haven't received the goods yet.
It should have arrived by now.
We're very worried about the situation.

That's strange; it was despatched on Monday.
I've checked with the driver.
He says that he delivered it on Tuesday.
Apparently, Mr Carlos signed for it.

We apologise for any inconvenience which this might have caused.
We'd like to apologise for not delivering the goods on time.
Please accept our apologies.
We're very sorry about this.

Don't worry; it really doesn't matter.
Please don't apologise; it was no trouble.
There is really no need to apologise.
That's, OK. No problem.

You really should have let us know sooner.
You ought to have made the situation clear.
You could have called us.
We understand your position, but please make sure that it doesn't happen again.

UNIT 15 Service industries

Preparation

Prepare to talk about the catering facilities where you work/study. Are they good, bad, indifferent? Does your organisation use outside caterers?

This unit develops the language covered in Unit 13. Information on other services which you have researched for that unit will be useful here.

Refer to the unit Language Notes and Useful Phrases on page 72.

1 Overview

Key dialogues

Listen to the exchanges and answer the questions.

a What sort of customer base does the company have?
   What is the ABL deal worth?
b What service does the company provide?
   What savings are they hoping for?
c What do they charge for recovering debts?
   Do they provide any other services?
d How many people do they employ?
   How is their record on hygiene and quality control?

2 Practice

Researching a catering service

Work in pairs. Refer to the audioscript for **1 Overview** for some useful language.

Partner A: You are thinking of using Emba. After asking around, you have obtained the information opposite. Contact **Partner B**, who has used Emba before, and ask about:

- number of employees
- training policies
- whether they advise on in-service catering facilities.

Partner B: Your information is on page 135.

EMBA *Catering ...*

❖ operates more than 220 contracts in the south and south-west, ranging in size from providing lunch for five, to complex operations for big employers such as Kaz Gas and the Mastor Bank for 2000 to 3000 staff.

❖ serves 75,000 meals a day

❖ is one of eight autonomous companies within a group with a combined turnover of more than $560 million a year.

3 Language focus

Refer to the language notes on page 72 when completing these exercises.

Correcting misunderstandings

1 Using the information about Emba Catering, practise correcting misunderstandings. Work in pairs.

They told me that … He/She said that … According to their sales people … Apparently … They were sure that …	Are you sure he/she said that … They must have said/meant … They wouldn't have said … I must have misunderstood … That can't be right. I need to check.

2 Write a message in which you check that you have understood information correctly.

e.g. It says in your brochure that you can supply ten contractors, but I have heard that this is not true any more. Also I read that …

Jobs in service industries

3 Write jobs which go with these service industries. Refer to your dictionary if you need to.

e.g. law ..*solicitor, lawyer, judge*..........

a insurance ....
b bank ....
c stock market ....
d dentistry ....
e medicine ....
f hotel industry ....
g police ....
h fire service ....
i information and communication technology (ICT) ....
j security ....
k catering ....

Fees and charges

4 Choose words from the box to complete the sentences. Refer to the examples in the Language Notes (page 72).

▸ fee	▸ charge	▸ commission	▸ expenses
▸ quote	▸ rates	▸ figure	▸ estimate

a They charge a one-off .... of €500.
b Our Turkish agent works on a .... basis.
c We have just received a bill for their travel ....
d Could you .... for five days work?
e We .... that the total will be $5000.
f Are your .... the same as last year's?
g It was a much higher .... than we expected.
h How much do you .... for a weekly service?

4 Listening

Identifying service industries

Match the speakers with the service industries.

a Speaker 1   i   insurance
b Speaker 2   ii law firm
c Speaker 3   iii newspaper recycling
d Speaker 4   iv IT consultancy
e Speaker 5   v   stockbroking

Reasons for choosing a supplier

1 Read the text, then answer the questions below it.

Pallet company collects empties and saves thousands

A company is offering industry major savings on the cost of pallets – the wooden platforms on which everything from cornflakes to computers is transported.

Up to now, companies have had two choices: to buy new pallets and see their stock diminish by theft, loss or damage; or to hire from a specialist company that collects and returns the empty pallets after use.

Makara Pallets, specialists in re-conditioning, now offer user companies a third choice.

They supply reconditioned pallets to the factory, collect the empties, separate any that are damaged, and return them to the depot to be repaired in a purpose-built workshop. The user pays a fixed price for continuous guaranteed supply.

Makara's first customer for the scheme is a company carrying its produce of bulk plastic packaging on thousands of pallets every week.

They hope to save more than 30% of the cost by using reconditioned pallets. The deal will be worth more than $500,000 to Makara.

'This is recycling at its best,' said Joint Managing Director Martin Myskov. 'It is possible only because we have expanded, with three new depots – and three more planned in the new year.

'Every pallet that arrives is individually sorted and graded to meet the varying demands of customers.

'Companies seeking quality approval need a pallet source they can rely on, not a street supplier. Unsafe pallets can cause serious damage to goods, and make a whole load unsafe.'

Makara plans to extend its collection service to a number of other countries soon.

a What is new about Makara's service?
b What problems can arise from buying new pallets?
c What kind of saving does Makara's first customer hope to make?
d How much is the deal worth?
e What can be the result of using unsafe pallets?

2 Note down your reasons for choosing suppliers. Do you make decisions based on price, quality, reliability, environmental/ethical factors, geographical location, etc.? Discuss your reasons with other members of the group.

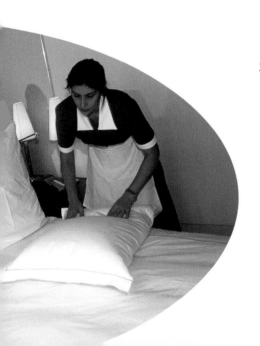

LANGUAGE REFERENCE

Language notes

For more detailed notes, see the Business Grammar Guide.

Fees and charges

Note the following examples.

e.g. Could you give us a quote for …?
How much do you charge for this kind of work?
You say there's no extra charge for …?
Does that figure include commission?
Our commission is 1.5%.
My fee is £2000 per day, plus expenses.
I'm afraid our rates have gone up.
We charge interest on overdue accounts.

Some service industry jobs

clerks	consultants
managers	analysts
dentists	guards
doctors	chefs
nurses	cooks
surgeons	waiters/waitresses
receptionists	solicitors
police officers	lawyers
fire officers	judges

Useful phrases

Our company has more than 200 contracts in the south-west.
These range in size from small to very large.
We have some big customers such as KAZ and Mastor.

We'd like you to give us a quote.
How much do you charge for this kind of work?
Could you let us know your fees?
Can I check that your commission is still 1.5%?

Makara are specialists in recycling.
Companies pay a fixed price for a guaranteed supply of materials.
We hope to save more than 30% by using reconditioned pallets.

I hear that they have a combined turnover of £360 million.
Apparently, they employ 2000 staff.
According to their sales people, the deal with Makara is worth $300 million.

They can't have said that.
They wouldn't have said that.
They must have meant $300,000.
You must have misunderstood.
They may have made a mistake.

The company has a strong ethical policy.
Price is not their main consideration when choosing a supplier.
They are very demanding.
They require a fast response if there are problems.

UNIT 16 Looking after visitors

1 Overview

Key dialogues

Listen to the dialogues and answer the questions.

a Why don't they take visitors sightseeing more often?
Do they ever take clients to a club in the evening?

b Does he have to take a gift?
What should he wear?

c How does the visitor feel about going to the opera?
Why is Tuesday difficult?

d What time are they going to meet?
Is there anything she can't eat?

Preparation

Be prepared to discuss:

- which types of hospitality are appropriate for different visitors
- which types of hospitality you have most enjoyed or have received
- special features of your region which you like to introduce to visitors
- food, sights, festivals, events, etc.

Refer to page 76 for this unit's Language Notes and Useful Phrases.

2 Practice

Planning an evening out

In pairs, talk about going out for the evening. **Partner A** is the host. **Partner B** is the guest. Refer to the Language Notes (page 76) for uses of *prefer* and *would rather*.

Planning

I thought we might …
I was thinking of …
Or would you rather …?
What would you prefer?
When would suit you?

→

I would love to.
I don't mind. / I'm easy.
I was hoping to …
I'm free every evening except …

Diet considerations

Is there anything you can't eat?

→

I don't eat [pork].
I can't have [anything with sugar in it].
I'm not allowed [dairy products].
I'm on a [gluten-free] diet.
I'm [(a) Muslim], so …
I'm allergic to …

Etiquette

It's (not) a good idea to …
You don't have to …
You needn't … (but …)
I would …

→

What should I wear?
Should I take/bring a gift?
What do you suggest I take/bring?
Should I arrive on time or [30 minutes] late/early?

Refer to the Language Notes on page 76 when completing these exercises.

mustn't, needn't *and* don't have to

1 Write *mustn't, needn't* or *don't have to* in the following sentences.

   a We .... arrive late.

   b You .... hurry, there's plenty of time.

   c It's an informal occasion, so you .... wear a suit.

   d You .... leave a tip, but I would.

   e I .... forget to invite Mario.

   f You .... come if you don't want to.

   g I .... eat anything with sugar in it – I'm a diabetic.

   h We .... finish the work till next week.

was/were going/hoping/planning to, *etc.*

2 Complete these sentences.

   e.g. I was thinking of ...*leaving now.*............. .
       Do you have to? It's very early.

   a – I was going/hoping/planning to ....
       – That would be nice.

   b – I was thinking of getting ....
       – I'd like that very much.

   c – We were hoping to ....
       – That's a very expensive place.

   d – I was planning to ....
       – Good idea. It was a great film.

3 Practise giving invitations. Work in pairs.

   e.g. – Are you free [on Friday night]?
       – Yes, I am. / No, I'm (afraid I'm) not. Why?
       – I was going/hoping/planning to … thinking of …
       – I'd like that … / Oh, what a pity. I would have enjoyed that.

4 Listening

Deciding where to go

1 Listen to the conversation. Where does the speaker take visitors when they are in Monaco? Complete the table.

2 How do the ideas discussed compare with the way that you entertain visitors in your company? What cultural considerations do you take into account when deciding where to take your visitors? Compare notes with a partner.

	Usually	**Occasionally**	**Rarely**
To lunch in a local restaurant			
To dinner in the centre			
Sightseeing			
To a football match			

Cultural sensitivities

1 Read the 'dos' and 'don'ts' for doing business with Japanese people. If you are Japanese, or if you have experience of doing business with Japanese business partners, is there anything you do not agree with?

Do

- ... sound supportive of all your company's products – even products that compete with those you are representing. To the Japanese, your loyalty to the company's overall operations is paramount.

- ... find out beforehand how long a meeting is scheduled to last. Often, the Japanese schedule an hour and it is tricky to exit earlier – and even if you do, you may not have gone beyond lengthy preliminaries.

- ... carry your business cards at all times – and remember that, in exchanging cards, you should offer your card first if the person you are meeting outranks you.

- ... let your host take you to the lift after meeting; he will feel he has not been fully hospitable if you suggest it is unnecessary.

Don't

- ... interrupt your host. The Japanese take a while to find the right words even in Japanese: if you interrupt a significant pause, you may miss an important point.

- ... show up late. Foreigners have an excuse in Tokyo, but if you really want to demonstrate you understand their market, do what the Japanese do and show up five minutes early.

- ... sound boastful about your company or your products. Let facts speak for themselves. Your products can, for instance, be effectively boosted by quoting what other people say about them.

- ... write on, or play with, your host's business card. Even for something as practical as noting some missing information, for instance, it is more diplomatic to let him write it on his card himself.

Giving advice

2 Make a list of cultural 'dos' and 'don'ts' for foreigners who are planning to do business with your company, people in your country, etc. Discuss the list with a partner.

> **Useful language**
>
> Never … / Always … It is/isn't a good idea to …
> You must never/always … It is best (not) to …
> You should never/always … Make sure you (don't) …
> If I were you, I would …
> Why don't you …?
> I (always) recommend …
> You don't need to …

LANGUAGE REFERENCE

Language notes

For more detailed notes, see the Business Grammar Guide.

mustn't, needn't (don't need to) and *don't have to*

We use *needn't (don't need to)* and *don't have to* for optional points.

e.g. You don't have to take a gift.
     You needn't wear a suit.

We use *mustn't* for essential points.

e.g. You mustn't be late.
     I mustn't miss the train.

prefer and *would rather*

Note the following examples of invitations.

e.g. Would you prefer to go to the theatre or …?
     Would you rather go out to dinner or …?
     What would you prefer to do?
     Where would you rather go?

Note the following examples of responses.

e.g. I'd prefer to go to a cinema.
     I'd rather go somewhere nearby.
     I'd prefer not to be too late.
     I'd rather not go out tonight.

was/were going/planning to/thinking of, etc.

These can be used for:

– changed plans

e.g. I was going/hoping/planning to invite you to dinner, but I had to go on a business trip.
     I was thinking of buying a bigger house, but decided I couldn't afford it.

– tentative suggestions and invitations

e.g. – Were you planning to do anything tomorrow night?

  – Not really, no.
  – I was thinking of going to see a film.
  – That sounds like a good idea.

Useful phrases

Where do you usually take your foreign clients?
Do you ever take them sightseeing?
Not often.   Very rarely.
We occasionally take them to the theatre.
We sometimes arrange a short boat trip for them.

Were you planning to do anything tomorrow night?
I was thinking of getting some tickets to the opera.
I was going to invite you out to dinner.
Would you rather go to a football match?
I'd prefer to go bowling.
I'm free every evening except Tuesday.

What should I wear tomorrow evening?
What's the dress code?
Should I bring a gift?

It's an informal occasion.
You needn't wear a suit.
You don't have to bring a gift, but I'm sure it would be appreciated.
We mustn't be late.

Always shake hands when you are introduced.
It's a good idea to carry your business cards.
It's best not to ask any personal questions.

Is there anything you don't eat?
Yes, I don't eat pork.
I can't have anything with sugar in it.
I'm vegetarian.   I'm diabetic.
I'm on a diet.   I'm allergic to seafood.
I love Lebanese food.

UNIT 17 Hotels and restaurants

Preparation

Bring to the class information on your favourite restaurants and hotels, brochures, menus, advertising material, etc.

Do you have any good restaurant and hotel anecdotes? Have you had any particularly good or bad experiences?

Refer to the Language Notes and Useful Phrases on page 80 of this unit.

1 Overview

Key dialogues

Listen to the exchanges and answer the questions.

a Where are they?
  What did she say to John?
b Is this their first drink?
  How would he like to pay for the drinks?
c What food do they order?
  What do they have to drink?

2 Practice

Entertaining guests in a hotel

1 Look at some stages of an evening out in a hotel. In pairs or small groups, put them in order, and discuss what people do and say at each stage. Is there anything else you would add to the list?

a Ask for the bill. ☐
b Attract the waiter's attention and order the food. ☐
c Check how your guests are going to get home. ☐
d Ask for your table. ☐
e Collect your coats and bags. ☐
f Make a toast. ☐
g Meet in the hotel lobby and suggest a drink in the bar. ☐
h Leave a tip. ☐
i Order a round of drinks. ☐
j Ask your guest to sit down (suggesting a seating arrangement). ☐
k Say goodnight and thank you. ☐

l Suggest moving to the restaurant. ☐
m When the food arrives, ask people to start. ☐
n Leave your coats and briefcases with the porter. ☐

2 In pairs or small groups, practise short conversations which might take place at different stages of an evening out.

Refer to the Language Notes as you complete these exercises.

Reported speech

1 Change the questions and statements into reported speech.

e.g. Have you stayed at this hotel before?

He asked me ...*if I had stayed at the*......

hotel before.

a They have excellent conference facilities.
He said ....

b Ask for a room with a sea view.
He told me ....

c I'll have the beef.
She said ....

d Don't order the fish. It isn't very good here.
He advised me ....

e We went out for lunch yesterday.
They said ....

f We are all going out for dinner tomorrow night.
Ralph said ....

g How much do you usually tip?
He asked ....

say/tell *and* speak/talk

2 Complete these examples with *say*, *tell*, *speak* or *talk*. In some cases, there is more than one possibility.

a I .... Dan to arrange everything.
b I .... , 'Don't wait until tomorrow.'
c Can you .... to your boss about it?
d We need to .... about it.
e I .... a little Polish, but not much.
f Let's .... about it in the morning.
g What did they .... to you?
h Can I .... to Mary, please?

Now work in pairs. Read the extracts from *The Little Book of Business Etiquette*, then tell your partner about what you have read. Do you agree with the article?

Partner A: Your extract is opposite.
Partner B: Your extract is on page 135.

As a general rule, the person who invites someone else to a business meal should pay. There are exceptions to this rule, however.

Example: An employer asks a manager for lunch to discuss a work-related issue. The manager in this situation would pick up the tab, unless the employee insists.

Example: A customer asks a salesperson to join him for dinner, and the topic of discussion is strictly business. The salesperson is justified in incurring the meal as a business expense.

From *The Little Book of Business Etiquette*, by Michael C. Thomsett

> **Useful language**
>
> It says that if/when you …
> It states that if/when you …
> It also says …
> Does it say who pays when/if …?
> What does it say about …?
> It doesn't mention …

Hotel and restaurant vocabulary

3 Which words in the box relate to a restaurant, which to a hotel reception, and which to a hotel room? (Some can be used more than once.)

▶ menu	▶ receptionist	▶ waiter
▶ bill	▶ shower	▶ laundry
▶ porter	▶ balcony	▶ view
▶ fish	▶ receipt	▶ double glazing
▶ counter	▶ reservation	▶ check-out
▶ desk	▶ booking	▶ wash basin

a restaurant: *menu, reservation*..................

b hotel reception: ....

c hotel room: ....

Discuss any recent experiences you have had in hotels and restaurants – good/bad meals and service, for example.

Ordering a meal

1 Listen to the conversation and refer to the menu. What do the speakers order?
2 Practise ordering from this menu or other menus which you have brought to the lesson.

	Starter	**Main course**
Ralph	onion soup	
Mary		
Hiroshi		

MINSTER RESTAURANT

INTRODUCING OUR NEW CHEF

Robert trained as a chef in Quimper, France and has worked as a chef in Lille and London. Look out for exciting changes to the menu which Robert will be making in the near future!

Lunch menu

Fresh fruit platter
A selection of sliced seasonal fruits with a choice of minted yoghurt dressing, or tropical sorbet

Smoked ham and strawberries

Smoked salmon

Baked cep mushrooms
Topped with a gratinée of mussels and shrimps glazed with cheese

Prawn salad
Prawns on a bed of mixed leaves

French onion soup

Sirloin steak
Served with a choice of spicy herb butter or green peppercorn sauce

Beef teriyaki
Slivers of beef fillet with mushrooms

Chicken peri peri
Barbequed spicy chicken breast, marinated with fresh chilli

Mixed seafood grill
Served with a Bernaise sauce
(Check with your waiter for today's selection.)

Pacific tiger prawns
Served in the shell with your choice of garlic or lemon butter sauce.

Vegetarian dish of the day

The above dishes are served with a selection of fresh seasonal vegetables, new potatoes, french fries or pilaff rice

Don't forget to look at our 'Daily specials' board.

Apple pie   Fresh fruit salad

A selection of ice cream   Chocolate mousse

LANGUAGE REFERENCE

Language notes

For more detailed notes, see the Business Grammar Guide.

Toasts and tipping

Note these phrases for making a toast.

e.g. Cheers!
Here's to the new project.
Your very good health!
I'd like to propose a toast to …

Note these phrases for leaving a tip.

e.g. Should I leave a tip?
Do you usually leave a tip?
Is service included?
Is 10% enough (as a tip)?

Some examples of reported speech

Reporting statements:

'We have excellent facilities.'
He said (that) they had/have excellent facilities.
'I'll make the bookings.'
She told me (that) she would make the bookings.
'I'll call you tomorrow.'
He said (that) he would call me the following day/tomorrow.
'I stayed there last year.'
He said (that) he had stayed there the year before.

Reporting questions:

'Where is the restaurant?'
I asked him where the restaurant was/is.
'Can you recommend a starter?'
He asked me If I could recommend a starter.
'Should we leave a tip?'
They wanted to know if they should leave a tip.
'Do you have any vacancies?'
They asked me whether we had/have any vacancies.

Making requests and giving advice:

'Please bring us the bill.'
We asked the receptionist to bring the bill.
'Don't have the soup.'
I advised him (not) to have the soup.

say/tell and speak/talk

Note the following examples of say.

e.g. What did he say to you?
He said (that) she'd be late.

Note the following examples of tell.

Could you tell me the time, please?
They told us not to wait.

Note the following examples of speak.

e.g. We need to speak to our lawyer about this.
Do you speak Arabic?
Please speak more slowly – I can't understand.

Note the following examples of talk.

e.g. Who was the person you were talking to?
Mauro talks a lot!

Useful phrases

Would you like a drink in the bar before we eat?
That's a good idea.
Where can we leave our coats?
There's a cloakroom in the lobby.

Do you have a reservation?
Yes, I booked a table for eight o'clock.
It's in the name of Tomasov.

Excuse me, we're ready to order.
I'd like the rump steak, please.
And how would you like your steak?
Medium rare.   Rare.   Well done.

I'll have the prawn salad for my starter.
Can I have the salad as a main course?
Is there a vegetarian option?

Let's start.   Cheers everyone!
Good luck with the project!
How's your meal?
It's very good. How's yours?
It's excellent.

Did you speak to John?
Did you talk to him about booking the hotel?
Yes I did. He said it had excellent conference facilities.
He told me to book a room with a sea view.
I also asked the receptionist to suggest a good local restaurant.

So what does the article say?
It says that if you invite someone out for a meal, you should pay the bill.
How much does it say you should tip?
It says you should tip about 10%.
In some situations, it's a good idea to split the bill.

UNIT 18 Corporate entertaining

1 Overview

Key dialogues

Listen and answer the questions.

a Why does she recommend the tournament?
What does the standard package include?

b What is special about the event?
Does the hospitality company have a good location?

c What hospitality package does the caller want?
Does she want an alternative to the standard package?

d What game do you think they are watching?
Do you think they are paying much attention to the game?

Preparation

You may not be personally involved in corporate entertaining, but this section covers a range of business-related social language.

Be prepared to talk about how your company or organisation entertains its visitors.

Bring in any brochures which you are able to collect from hospitality companies. What would be your ideal hospitality package if you were being entertained?

Refer to the unit Language Notes and Useful Phrases on page 84.

2 Practice

Booking hospitality

In pairs, practise booking a hospitality package. Decide on an event.

e.g. a tennis tournament
a race meeting
a football match
an open air concert

Partner A: You work for a hospitality company.

Partner B: You are interested in taking clients to the event. Your information is on page 135.

Useful phrases

Can I make a suggestion?
I would recommend taking them to a sports event.
I think you should book it now.
You could move it to the following day.
Have you thought of having live music?
Why not have a buffet instead?
How about booking the tickets tomorrow?
If I were you, I'd discuss it with [Keith].

Refer to the Language Notes on page 84 as you do these exercises.

Spelling and position of adverbs

1 Change the adjectives to adverbs and put them in these sentences.

e.g. I agree with you.

(total) ...*I totally agree with you.*...

a The reception went well.
(extreme) ....

b I read the information.
(quick) ....

c We take visitors to the theatre.
(rare) ....

d I drove to work this morning.
(slow) ....

e Driving conditions were difficult.
(terrible) ....

f She organised everything.
(brilliant) ....

g She didn't forget anything.
(surprising) ....

Comparative adverbs

2 Put these adverbs into the comparative form.

e.g. When we have the right team, the event runs
(smoothly) ...*even more smoothly.*...

a If you want to get to work on time, you should get
up (early) ....

b We have to work (hard) .... because
we're a small team.

c Sales rose (slowly) .... in the
second quarter.

d He is no good in a team – he works (well)
.... on his own.

e I pay about once a month – I used to pay
(often) ....

f You drive (badly) .... than I do.

g I really need your reply (soon) ....
than that.

Sports vocabulary

3 Which sports might the phrases below relate to?
(Each phrase can relate to more than one sport.)

▸ snooker	▸ boxing	▸ wrestling	▸ swimming
▸ golf	▸ badminton	▸ table tennis	▸ squash
▸ football	▸ sailing	▸ rugby	▸ motor racing

a They're playing well.
...*football*...   ...*rugby*...   ....

b Good shot!
....

c It wasn't a very good fight.
....

d Well played!
....

e Did you enjoy the match?
....

f It was a very close race.
....

g What a terrible pass!
....

h Which round is it?
....

i The first half was better.
....

4 Which are your favourite sports? Which sports
do you prefer to play? Which sports would you
rather watch?

4 | Application

Tailoring a hospitality package

1 Listen to a client booking hospitality at a golf tournament. Note down the changes to the standard package which she requires and any special requests?

The client doesn't require floral arrangements.

....

....

....

BURWALL
HOSPITALITY

The deluxe hospitality package includes:

- a luxury air-conditioned suite for clients
- floral arrangements
- a cordoned-off area with comfortable seating
- an excellent view of the proceedings
- toilet facilities
- admission charges

- private parking facilities, and
- souvenir programmes.

Superb catering to include:

- morning coffee
- a full four-course lunch
- afternoon tea
- full bar facilities, and
- music to accompany meals, by arrangement.

2 Read the extract from a brochure. Then answer the questions. Would you use the Skyhigh Club to entertain your clients or customers?

a Why will it be easy for visitors to find the club?

b How long does the flying display last?

c Is there more than one hospitality complex?

d What, in your opinion, is the strongest selling point in the extract?

The Skyhigh Club

The club is located within the main hospitality complex. It is centrally located, giving a superb and uninterrupted view of the flying display. It is also conveniently located close to all the other show attractions.

Experienced management

The club will run as a private suite where parties of between two and 50 can be catered for, at tables seating ten guests. Your guests will be greeted on arrival and escorted to the Skyhigh Club, where they will be met by the Skyhigh reception team. An experienced manager will be in the club at all times to ensure your day runs smoothly.

Special access

Your guests will arrive by special VIP routes with a separate entrance to the airfield. Full details with maps and passes will be sent in June.

Event information

Airfield opens	8am
Exhibition and Fun Park open	9am
Arena displays commence	9.30am
Flying displays commence	2pm
Flying display finale ends	6pm
Arena displays finish	7pm
Exhibition and Fun Park close	7.30pm
Airfield closes	8pm

LANGUAGE REFERENCE

Language notes

For more detailed notes, see the Business Grammar Guide.

Adverbs

Most adjectives:

quick → quickly
careful → carefully

Adjectives ending in -le:

possible → possibly
profitable → profitably

Adjectives ending in -ic:

automatic → automatically
realistic → realistically

Adjectives ending in -y:

easy → easily
temporary → temporarily

Common exceptions:

hard → hard
early → early
public → publicly
long → long
little → little

Examples:

We ensure that everything runs smoothly.
I completely disagree.
She hardly ever takes time off work.
Everything went extremely well.
Their prices are fairy high.
He earns very little.

Comparative adverbs

Short adverbs:

hard → harder
soon → sooner
early → earlier

Longer adverbs:

frequently → more frequently
efficient → more efficiently

Common exceptions:

well → better
badly → worse
little → less

Examples:

He has been working here longer than me.
It runs more smoothly now.
We need a decision faster than that.
The sooner, the better.

Useful phrases

What time does it start?
The event begins at 10am and lasts for four hours.
Our room is located in the main hospitality complex.
We are reasonably close to all the attractions.
We have a superb view of the proceedings.

The package we provide includes a four-course lunch.
a full buffet   souvenir programmes
Our experienced team will ensure …
… that your day runs smoothly.
… that everything goes well.

Can I make a booking?
Yes, of course. When is it for?
I'd like to book the standard package.
Have you thought of having music?
Why don't you have a hot buffet lunch instead of a cold one?
I'm very keen on the idea of a hot buffet.
I'm not sure about having music.

I'll confirm the booking next week.
I'll try and let you know sooner than that, if possible.
I'll let you know earlier than that if I can.
We can arrange things more quickly, if necessary.
Let me know if you need to make any changes.

It's a very close race.
It's a very good game.
They're playing well.
Well played!
Good shot!

UNIT 19 Setting up meetings

1 Overview

Key dialogues

Listen to the exchanges and answer the questions.

a When are they meeting?
Can she meet later if necessary?

b Where is the meeting taking place?
Does the speaker want Jason to get back to her?

c What's the problem?
Has he received an agenda?

d Are they OK for the meeting on the 27th?
Will the plan to meet for lunch on Friday work?

Preparation

Think about the language you need to set up a meeting – the messages you send, the phone calls you make. What type of agendas do you prepare for the meetings you attend? Bring examples of formal/ informal agendas to the class for analysis.

Be prepared to talk about the meetings you attend and to introduce the agendas which you bring to the lesson.

Look at the Language Reference section for this unit on page 88.

2 Practice

Arranging a time and place to meet

1 Ramond Bagot is organising a meeting. He wants Phillip Lux to be present. Read the exchange of emails and write in when they were sent. Then write in the sender's and receiver's names.

   i 21 May, 10am
   ii 21 May, 3.30pm
   iii 22 May, 11am

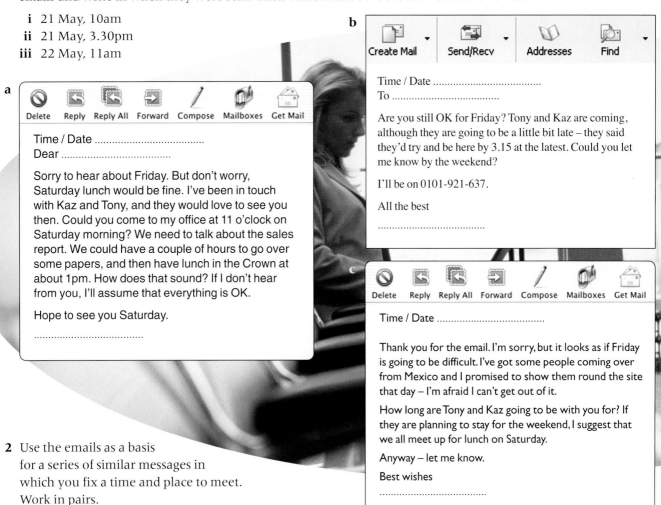

a

Delete · Reply · Reply All · Forward · Compose · Mailboxes · Get Mail

Time / Date ....
Dear ....

Sorry to hear about Friday. But don't worry, Saturday lunch would be fine. I've been in touch with Kaz and Tony, and they would love to see you then. Could you come to my office at 11 o'clock on Saturday morning? We need to talk about the sales report. We could have a couple of hours to go over some papers, and then have lunch in the Crown at about 1pm. How does that sound? If I don't hear from you, I'll assume that everything is OK.

Hope to see you Saturday.

....

b

Create Mail · Send/Recv · Addresses · Find

Time / Date ....
To ....

Are you still OK for Friday? Tony and Kaz are coming, although they are going to be a little bit late – they said they'd try and be here by 3.15 at the latest. Could you let me know by the weekend?

I'll be on 0101-921-637.

All the best

....

c

Delete · Reply · Reply All · Forward · Compose · Mailboxes · Get Mail

Time / Date ....

Thank you for the email. I'm sorry, but it looks as if Friday is going to be difficult. I've got some people coming over from Mexico and I promised to show them round the site that day – I'm afraid I can't get out of it.

How long are Tony and Kaz going to be with you for? If they are planning to stay for the weekend, I suggest that we all meet up for lunch on Saturday.

Anyway – let me know.

Best wishes

....

2 Use the emails as a basis for a series of similar messages in which you fix a time and place to meet. Work in pairs.

3 | Listening

Last-minute changes

Phillip Lux calls Ramond Bagot with a last-minute change of plan. Listen to the conversation and put the final details in the right order. Note the examples of *had better* in both the audioscript and Language Notes (page 88).

a Ramond gives Phillip a lift to a hotel near Heathrow. ☐
b Kaz and Tony fly from Heathrow. ☐
c Phillip flies to Belgium with the Mexican clients. [☐]
d The Mexican clients fly to Madrid direct from Brussels. ☐
e Kaz, Tony, Ramond and Phillip have lunch together. ☐
f Phillip flies to London. ☐

4 | Language focus

Look at the Language Notes on page 88 as you do these exercises.

be able to

1 Complete the sentences with *can* or *could* where possible. Where *can* and *could* aren't appropriate, use be *able to*.

e.g. Would you ...*be able to*... meet me on the 24th?

a I .... (not) take the minutes – I'll be away.
b Is she going to .... make the meeting?
c I'd like to .... type properly.
d We should .... meet on 27th.
e It look's as if we .... use room 207.
f I enjoy .... walk to the office.
g I .... (not) post it – it wasn't ready.
h You must .... reach him somehow.

look as if/though *and* sound as if/though

2 Change the sentences, using *look as if/though* and *sound as if/though*.

e.g. I think everyone can come.
It *looks as if/though everyone can come*.

a I have the impression that you don't agree.
You ....

b I think we'd better postpone the meeting.
It ....

c It seems that the room isn't available.
It ....

d I think you need a holiday.
You ....

e Your car seem to need repairing.
Your car ....

f His accent sounds Spanish.
He ....

Punctuation marks (vocabulary)

3 Match the punctuation marks with their names.

a	!	**i**	inverted commas
b	%	**ii**	exclamation mark
c	"	**iii**	question mark
d	-	**iv**	round brackets
e	*	**v**	stroke/oblique/slash
f	?	**vi**	percentage sign
g	[ ]	**vii**	square brackets
h	:	**viii**	full stop
i	,	**ix**	comma
j	.	**x**	colon
k	( )	**xi**	semi-colon
l	;	**xii**	dash
m	/	**xiii**	asterisk

Agendas

1 Which of these agendas is more familiar to you? Compare them with the agendas you use.

> 1) Department reports
>
> 2) Cooperation with OIB
>
> 3) Update on ISO project
>
> 4) Report on new computer system
>
> 5) AOB

Agenda

Management Meeting
Room 406, Volta House
at 10am on 24 July

1 Apologies for absence.
2 Minutes of the last meeting.
3 Matters arising from the minutes.
4 Monthly sales report and development budget (enclosed).
5 Research and development budget (enclosed).
  a Report by Finance Committee (enclosed).
  b Review.
6 Any other business.
7 Date of next meeting.

Three enclosures: Monthly sales report

Research and development budget for next year
Report on projected R&D spending

Rearranging a meeting

2 In small groups, draw up an agenda. Agree on the items. Refer to the Useful Language box.

3 Now set up a meeting.

  a Fix a time and place.
  b Notify everyone.
  c Circulate the agenda.
  d Rearrange the time and/or place. (Someone has a change of plan.)
  e Call to check that everyone can make it.

4 Write an email in which you confirm the details of the meeting and refer to the agenda.

> **Useful language**
>
> Are you (still) OK for …?
> It's taking place at [2pm] on …
> We're meeting to discuss …
> I'll send you a copy of the agenda.
> I'm having some problems at this end.
> The meeting has been put off till …
> It looks as if [Friday] is going to be difficult.
> Would you be able to meet at/on …?
> We'd better meet on/at … instead.

LANGUAGE REFERENCE

Language notes

For more detailed notes, see the Business Grammar Guide.

had better

Note the following examples.

e.g. I'd (I had) better check with my boss.
We'd (We had) better postpone the meeting.
You'd (You had) better not mention that.
Had he better call to confirm? No, it's not necessary.
Had we better meet at the airport instead?
Yes. we'd better. / Yes, we had.

Some uses of *to be able to*

Note how we use *be able to* instead of *can* and *could*.

e.g. I wasn't able to get there in time.
(I couldn't get there in time.)
She isn't able to attend the meeting.
(She can't attend the meeting.)

Note how we use the infinitive form.

e.g. He'd like to be able to attend the conference.
We should be able to make a decision then.

Note how we use the *-ing* form.

e.g. I enjoy being able to walk to work.
It's hard to get a job here without being able to drive.

Punctuation: some useful phrases:

The heading should be underlined.
That phrase should be in italics/capitals.
That word begins with a capital letter.
That sentence should be in inverted commas.
Leave a line.
Begin at the margin.
New paragraph. Next line.
My web address is wwwdotenglish4dotcom
(www.english4.com)
My email address is ab at marshallcavendish dot com
(ab@marshallcavandish.com)

Rearranging a meeting

Note the following phrases.

e.g. Could we postpone the meeting until Friday?
Could we put it off till the end of the week?

We could move it to next week.
Is it possible to change the date?
It has been moved to the boardroom.
It has been delayed till 3.15.
We'll have to cancel the meeting.
We'll have to call it off.

Useful phrases

When's the meeting?
It's in the morning on Friday the 23rd.
We're meeting at ten o'clock.
It's taking place at Volta House.
We're holding the meeting in room 406.

We're meeting to talk about the new contract.
And we also need to discuss the sales report.
I'll send you a copy of the agenda.

Are you still OK for the 27th?
Can you still make the meeting?
Could you let me know by the weekend at the latest if there is a problem?

I have some problems with the date you've suggested.
It looks as if Friday is going to be difficult.
It looks like the room isn't available.

I thought I'd better call you.
We'd better postpone the meeting.
We need to set up another meeting.
We'd better meet on Friday instead of Tuesday.
I'm sorry about this.

Would you be able to join us for lunch?
Is Rose going to be able to come too?
I suggest that we all meet at my place at 12.30.
If I don't hear from you, I'll assume that everything is OK.

The seminar has been put off till Thursday.
It's now been scheduled to start at 3.15.
It's been moved to the boardroom.

UNIT 20 Meeting procedures

1 Overview

Key dialogues

Listen and answer the questions.

a What is the main purpose of the meeting? Does everyone have an agenda?
b Why is the speaker concerned about the article in *The Tribune*?
Why does the speaker argue for a more realistic PR budget?
c Do smokers support the ban? What were the findings of the union survey?
d Does the meeting approve the proposals? Does anyone abstain?

Preparation

Think about the meetings you attend. Do you have any particular difficulties when putting your point across, agreeing, disagreeing?

Come to the lesson prepared to take part in a simulated meeting and to explore any areas of language which you find difficult.

Note that there are some phrases which can be used in meetings on pages 135–136.

Refer to page 92 of this unit, and study the Language Notes and Useful Phrases.

2 Talking points

Meeting targets

1 Read the quotes.

Meetings: some quotes

- 'I used to have a great job; now I have meetings.'

- 'Avoid large meetings; they don't work. If you get stuck in one, that's bad management.'

- 'If you haven't made up your mind what to do in the first five minutes of a meeting, you probably never will. The rest of the meeting is merely to prepare the niceties, allow everyone their say and preserve the idea that it's been considered, democratically arrived at.'

- 'It's at the end of a meeting when the best ideas come out. People drop their guard and you can ask them what they really think.'

- 'Conduct your meetings at a round table, the way they do at Hitachi. You get better participation because there's no sense of hierarchy. Also at certain Unilever companies, they reserve the last five minutes of every meeting for a general discussion on the usefulness of the meeting itself. That's a great idea.'

- 'Meetings are indispensable, especially when you don't want to do anything.'

- 'Two hours are enough. If satellites can circle the world in 89 minutes, you can surely run a board meeting in 120.'

2 Which of the views do you agree with? Which views do you disagree with?

3 Write a statement or quote that represents your views on meetings.

From an article by Jeffrey Robinson

3 Language focus

Refer to the Language Notes on page 92 as you work through these exercises.

Second Conditional

1 Rewrite the following sentences using the Second Conditional.

e.g. We don't have enough time. We'll have to end the meeting now.

   If we had more time, we wouldn't have to end the meeting now.

a We don't pay them enough. They are going to go on strike.

   ....

b We should pay off our bank loans. Then we won't have the bank after us.

   ....

c I would organise a weekly meeting, but I'm not in charge.

   ....

d We don't have accreditation. Our customers will stop buying from us.

   ....

e We don't get any work done. We have too many meetings.

   ....

f We spend too much on entertaining clients. There is no money for training.

   ....

g They use the service – that's why they support it.

   ....

h You should take more exercise.

   ....

Agreement and disagreement

2 Do these phrases indicate agreement or disagreement? Which ones can be used neutrally?

	Agreement	Disagreement	Neutral
Absolutely.	✓		
That's not true.			
I'm not sure I agree with that.			
Definitely.			
I don't know.			
I don't agree with that.			
That's right.			
I'm afraid I disagree completely.			
I agree with you up to a point.			
I agree with most of what you say.			
Yes, but …			
Not necessarily.			

In pairs, use the phrases below and those in the table to practise agreeing, disagreeing and giving neutral responses.

I (don't) think/believe … In my opinion/view … I'm in favour of … I'm opposed to …		I'm afraid I don't agree. [Refer to the phrases above.]

e.g. – I believe we need to increase the marketing budget by 10%.
– I don't agree with that. Last year we spent …

4 Listening

Phrases used in meetings

Listen to the extracts from four meetings (a–d) and answer the questions.

a Had the people at the meeting met before?
  Why was the speaker late for the meeting?

b Who is taking the minutes?
  What is the purpose of the meeting?

c What are they taking about?
  Does Mark think the contractors are trustworthy?

d Is the proposal approved by the meeting?
  How does Janet vote?

5 Application

Meeting to discuss a ban on smoking

1 Read the article about smoking in the workplace. Do you agree with the policy? Make notes in preparation for a meeting to discuss the implications for your business.

Millions of smokers are wondering what awaits them when they return to work on Monday after a new law comes into effect at midnight tomorrow establishing non-smoking as the rule in all public places.

The law will have its most serious impact in offices and factories, where people will no longer be able to smoke anywhere on company premises.

Smoking has been banned in communal areas such as canteens and reception rooms for some years, but employers have been able to set aside special sections to accommodate their smokers. Many smokers have gathered outside office buildings when smoking has not been allowed inside. After the new law, this practice will also be banned.

'The main principle of the law is to protect non-smokers, We cannot ignore any longer the evidence of cancer caused by smoking and also passive smoking.'

Items for the agenda

- Company policy on smoking
- Counselling for smokers
- Resistance of smokers to the new laws
- Penalties for breaking the ban
- Sympathy for smokers?
- Positive action (anti-smoking posters, etc.)

2 Hold a meeting to discuss the proposed ban on smoking in all areas of the workplace. Refer to the article and to other documents which you have brought to the lesson. Arguments in favour of smoking can be found, for example, at www.forestonline.org

When referring to sections of a document, check the phrases in the Language Notes on page 92 to help you.

e.g. In the third paragraph, line 5, it says …
   It's in the third sentence …
   If you look at the third bullet point …

LANGUAGE REFERENCE

Language notes

For more detailed notes, see the Business Grammar Guide.

The Second Conditional

Affirmative:

I would come to the meeting if I had time.
If we new her number, we could call her.
If I were you, I'd check the figures.

Negative:

If I didn't like the job, I wouldn't stay.
If he couldn't drive, he would have to learn.
Most smokers would support the policy if they didn't smoke. If they didn't smoke, they wouldn't be smokers.

Interrogative:

Would it be more convenient if we started earlier?
Would they mind if we postponed the meeting?
What would happen if somebody was ill?

Short answers:

Yes, it would.   No, it wouldn't.
Yes, they would.   No, they wouldn't.

Referring to documents

Note the following phrases.

e.g. In the third paragraph, line five, it says …
In the fourth sentence down, it states …
In the next line, it refers to …
If you look at page four, there is a reference to …
… at the top/bottom of the second column …
… at the beginning/end of paragraph two …
… in the middle of column/paragraph one …
… just above/below that …
If you check the third bullet point …

Useful phrases

Shall we begin?
There's a lot to get through.
Has everyone got a copy of the agenda?
So, there are four main topics on the agenda.
Let's start with item 1.

Our main aim is to approve the budget increases.
Mark, what's your opinion?
I believe you wanted to say something about this.

As you know, I'm in favour of the plan.
I'm opposed to spending any more money.
I'm afraid I totally disagree.
I don't agree with what Mark said.

Can we deal with point 3 later?
Can we move on to the next item?
I'd like to summarise what we have agreed so far.

In the first line, it says smoking will be banned completely.
In the second paragraph, it only refers to a ban in 'enclosed areas'.
At the end of the second page that statement is repeated.

If we don't discuss this now, we'll never discuss it.
If we didn't spend so much on outside contractors, we'd have more money to do the work ourselves.
If I were you, I'd check the facts very carefully.

Shall we vote on the proposal?
Those in favour? Those against?
The motion is carried.
Thank you. I suggest we leave it there.

UNIT 21 Meeting follow-up

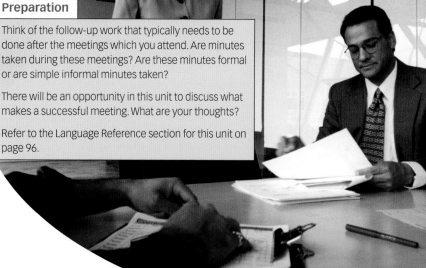

1 Overview

Key dialogues

Listen to the conversations and answer the questions.

a Why didn't the meeting start on time?
Did they get through the agenda?

b Did anyone take minutes?
What was decided about the security problem on the Tafari site?

c When is the next meeting with Veltex?
Did he send the proposal, as agreed?

d How is he getting on with the revised schedule?
What was Mr Awai's reaction to the revised schedule?

> **Preparation**
>
> Think of the follow-up work that typically needs to be done after the meetings which you attend. Are minutes taken during these meetings? Are these minutes formal or are simple informal minutes taken?
>
> There will be an opportunity in this unit to discuss what makes a successful meeting. What are your thoughts?
>
> Refer to the Language Reference section for this unit on page 96.

2 Practice

Follow-up to a meeting

1 Read the email. Is Fabio Mercotzi senior, junior or equal in position to Pilar Hernandez?

Delete | Reply | Reply All | Forward | Compose | Mailboxes | Get Mail | Junk

Hello Fabio

It was good to see you last week. I think that the meeting went very well, and that we managed to cover a lot of ground. I have already contacted the contractor as agreed, and I put your suggestions about delivery procedures to him.

He thought they were a good idea in principle. He suggested that we give them specific details of what we want, and they will draw up a plan for us to consider. I said you were sending them a more detailed outline of your proposals.

Not so much luck on the money question, though. They want to charge us for anything which was not in the original contract. But I haven't given up. I'm meeting their MD next week to discuss our credit limit, so I'll raise the matter then.

Hope you received the action steps. Looking forward to receiving the notes you promised on how to handle next week's meeting.

With best wishes

Pilar Hernandez

2 Tick the action steps in the memo below which are referred to in Pilar's email to Fabio.

MEMO

Site Manager Meeting

17 April

cc Fabio Mercotzi, Harry Gross, Pilar Hernandez

Action

● PH to contact NAK Supplies:
  – re. changes in delivery procedures
  – to enquire about price reductions.

● PH to arrange meeting with NAK's MD to discuss credit limits.

● FM to send a more detailed outline of proposals to NAK and HG.

● HG to check how the changes affect the insurance position.

● FM to send PH notes on handling the money questions.

3 | Listening

A follow-up phone call

1 Listen to the follow-up phone conversation between Pilar Hernandez and Fabio Mercotzi. Then answer the questions.

a Has Fabio received Pilar's email?
b What was Pilar expecting to receive from Fabio?
c Why hasn't Fabio sent anything?
d Will NAK be happy to make the changes for a small fee?
e Why does Harry Gross need a copy of the proposals?
f What does Pilar promise to do at the end of the call?

2 In pairs, practise short follow-up phone calls in which you need to clarify some matters. Refer to a meeting, emails, etc.

4 | Language focus

Refer to the Language Notes on page 96 as you work through the exercises.

More reported speech

1 Change the following sentences to indirect speech. Refer to the examples in Language Notes (page 96).

e.g. 'It would be a good idea if she circulated the agenda in advance.'

Max wanted ..*her to circulate the agenda in advance.*..

He suggested ..*that she should circulate the agenda in advance.*..

a 'I think Ali should chair the meeting.'

Anita said ....

She proposed ....

b 'Who is going to take the minutes?'

Ivan asked ....

He wanted ....

c 'Why don't we demand compensation?'

Lupe wondered ....

She suggested ....

d 'I think we should cancel the order.'

Franz thought ....

He proposed ....

Verbs followed by the infinitive

2 In pairs, talk about commitments and decisions, using the verbs in the box. Think of an example for each verb. Refer to meetings which you have attended.

I	agreed	to …
	arranged	
We	decided	not to …
	managed	
My assistant	offered	
	promised	
etc.	remembered	
	forgot	
	hoped	
	planned	

e.g. We didn't manage to get through the agenda yesterday, so we agreed to meet again tomorrow.

6 | Application

Checking action steps

In pairs or groups, decide on a number of actions to be taken following a meeting. See **2 Practice** for some examples. Then have a follow-up meeting to check on progress. Refer to the useful language in the box.

> **Useful language**
>
> Did you manage to …?
> Were you able to …?
> What's the position with/on …?
> How are you getting on with …?
> It's all taken care of.
> I'm hoping/planning to do it on …
> Which [document] was it?
> To be honest, I've been so busy …

5 | Talking point

Organising a successful meeting

1 Reflect on meetings you have attended. Then, from your point of view, number the list in order of importance for organising a successful meeting.
   (1 = most important.)

   ☐ plenty of notice
   ☐ comfortable chairs
   ☐ time limit
   ☐ agenda circulated in advance
   ☐ working documents circulated in advance
   ☐ the right time of day
   ☐ chance for everyone to speak
   ☐ a round table
   ☐ a limited number of people
   ☐ enough time
   ☐ good/firm chairperson
   ☐ coffee/refreshments
   ☐ no interruptions
   ☐ other – give examples.

2 Discuss your findings with the rest of the group. Can you agree on a 'top ten'?

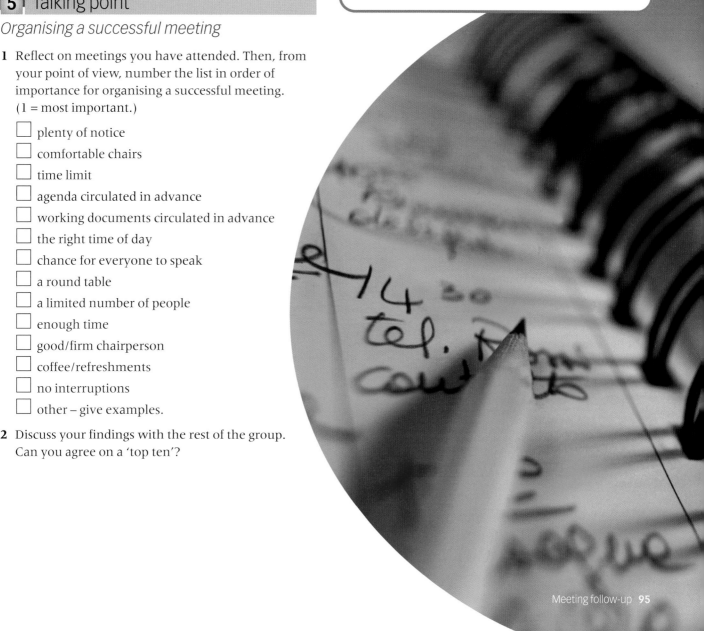

LANGUAGE REFERENCE

Language notes

For more detailed notes, see the Business Grammar Guide.

More reported speech

Note the following examples.

e.g. *'Will it be ready on time?'*

> She asked if it would be ready on time.
> She wondered if it would be ready on time.
> She wanted to know if it would be ready on time.

'I think we should hire a bigger room.'

> He said that we should hire a bigger room.
> He thought that we should hire a bigger room.
> He proposed that we should hire a bigger room.
> He suggested that we should hire a bigger room.

'Could you report back at the next meeting?'

> He asked her to report back at the next meeting.
> He told her to report back at the next meeting.
> He wants her to report back at the next meeting.

Verbs followed by the infinitive

We use infinitives with *to*:

– after many verbs such as *agree, arrange, decide, expect, forget, hope, manage, offer, need, plan, prefer, promise, try, want*

e.g. She **agreed to help** me.
> **Did** you **manage to fix up** an appointment?

(Note how the negative is formed:

e.g. I **decided not to go** to the conference.)

– after some adjectives such as *easy, difficult, good, great, important, necessary, common, quicker* (comparatives)

e.g. It's **good to see** you again.
> I found it **difficult to understand** him.

– for written action points following a meeting

e.g. GL **to contact** VJ.

Useful phrases

How did the meeting go?
Did you manage to get through the agenda?
Did the meeting overrun?

It went very well. We covered a lot of ground.
We didn't manage to discuss all the points,
We agreed to meet again next week.

Who chaired the meeting?
Who took the minutes?
Anita proposed that Vassos should chair the meeting.
Pilar suggested that Simon should take some notes.
Are you going to circulate the minutes?
I'll copy you all in.

What's the position with NAK?
Were you able to contact the contractor?
How are you getting on with the project?

I thought you were going to send me your proposals.
Did you remember to send a copy to the CEO?
To be honest, I'm not sure I did.
I've been so busy, I simply haven't had time.
I'm planning to do it tomorrow.

Lu managed to send the proposal, as agreed.
We've sent you the action points, as promised.
It's all taken care of.

When is the next meeting?
We arranged to meet again on the 11th.

UNIT 22 Arranging a visit

1 Overview

Key dialogues

Listen and answer the questions.

a What is the purpose of Faridah Khan's call?
  Will Dr Salem be visiting the new laboratory in Vermont?

b When is he visiting Sin Go Wan?
  Is the meeting with Greg Rice organised yet?

c When does his flight arrive in Kuala Lumpur?
  How long will he be staying in Singapore?

d Does she take the first or the third exit off the City Expressway?
  Note down the directions from Winchester Avenue to the hotel.

Preparation

Bring to the class any itineraries and messages concerning travel arrangements which you have prepared or which you have received.

Be prepared to talk about places you have been to and any business trips which you have made.

Refer to the Useful Phrases and Language Notes for this unit, which are on page 100.

2 Practice

Checking an itinerary

1 Work in pairs.

> **Partner A:** You receive a call from **Partner B**, who needs details of your forthcoming visit to Malaysia. Your information is included in the itinerary.
> **Partner B:** Your information is on page 136.

2 Write an email confirming the arrangements made.

Itinerary →→→→

23 Nov	Arrival at Kuala Lumpur airport. Flight LF 234 at 2.30pm
24 Nov	Visit to Zin Go Wan.
25 Nov	Transfer by car to Ipoh.
26 Nov	Meeting with Mr Brown.
27 Nov	Return to Kuala Lumpur airport. Singapore Airlines, flight SQ 739 at 11.30am to Singapore.

3 Language focus

Refer to the Language Notes on page 100 as you complete these exercises.

Talking about the future

1 Compare the meaning of the examples.

I'm leaving on Friday.
I'm going to leave on Friday.
I'll leave on Friday if I can get a flight.
The flight leaves at 6pm.
I'll be leaving on Friday.

2 Complete the sentences with an appropriate future form of the verb.
e.g. ..*They're going to*.. win the contract.

a .... to Budapest next week?
b .... if I can arrange it.
c What .... this afternoon?
d I .... some clients.
e When .... (leave)?
f I think they .... at about 5.30.
g I .... this afternoon.
h The last train .... at midnight.

The Future Continuous

3 Work in pairs. Find out what your partner will be doing:

- this time tomorrow
- this time next month
- this time next week
- this time next year
- in two years' time.

e.g. – Where do you think you'll be
working this time next year?
– I expect I'll still be working
in the bank.
– This time next week,
I'll be flying to
San Fransisco.

while, during *and* for

4 Compare these examples.

I will be in Boston <u>for</u> two days.
I hope we will meet <u>during</u> my stay.
My assistant will be here <u>while</u> I am away.

Now complete the sentences with *while, during* or *for*.
a Did you do much sightseeing .... you were there?
b We don't want any calls .... the meeting.
c Will you be seeing John .... you are in Paris?
d There were no trains .... three hours.
e She usually visits the States a couple of times .... the summer.
f Next month, I'll be working in Hungary .... two weeks.
g I don't like being contacted about work .... I'm on holiday.
h Will you have time to visit us .... your stay?

Future plans

5 Write about some future plans in your business or personal life.

e.g. I'll be leaving for Paris on Friday.
While I'm there I hope to visit our
new suppliers and I would also like
to spend some time sightseeing.
I'll send you an update.

4 | Reading

Preparing for a visit

1 Fill in the gaps in the text with the words below.

▸ on	▸ on	▸ in	▸ in	▸ with
▸ with	▸ for	▸ at	▸ to	▸ to

2 Now read the letter. What is the reason for Ms Braun's visit to the States?

rfm GmbH

OTTOSTRASSE 47, D4000 DUSSELDORF

Dr J. C. Keller
President
Blue Ribbon Inc
14940 Magnolia Blvd
Boston
MA91503 USA

Dear Dr Keller

I am writing **a** .... behalf of the managing director of RFM, Ms Rita Braun, to inform you that she will be visiting Boston **b** .... 11 and 12 July and that she would very much like to arrange an appointment **c** .... a member of your staff.

As our organisation also specialises **d** .... training for health and safety, Ms Braun is keen **e** .... discuss possible future cooperation **f** .... you. We are very interested **g** .... establishing a relationship with an American partner.

If you would like **h** .... meet Ms Braun, please let me know when would be most convenient **i** .... you.

Ms Braun will be staying **j** .... the Farrington Inn while she is in Boston.

Yours sincerely

Linda B. Gaddum

LINDA GADDUM
Personal Assistant

5 | Application

Directions from an airport

1 Listen to the recording, then put the taxi directions to the Farrington Inn in the correct order.

ATTN. Rita Braun

DIRECTIONS TO THE FARRINGTON INN FROM LOGAN AIRPORT

Thank you for deciding to stay with us while you are in Boston. Please call us as soon as you arrive here, especially if your plane is early or late. We look forward to meeting you.

BY TAXI

- Go down Harvard, and take your first left again, onto FARRINGTON AVE. ☐
- Follow the signs to ALLSTON. ☐
- Tell the cab driver to take the SUMNER TUNNEL, and then get on the EXPRESSWAY SOUTH, which takes you to the MASSACHUSETTS TURNPIKE (Mass Pike). ☑ 1
- We are the fifth house on the right, number 23. ☐
- Take the Mass Pike west to the first exit, signposted to ALLSTON-CAMBRIDGE. ☐
- Go to the fourth set of lights, and turn left. This is HARVARD AVE – there is an antique store on the corner. ☐

2 Work in pairs. **Partner A** gives directions to his/her workplace. **Partner B** takes notes. Check that the notes are accurate.

LANGUAGE REFERENCE

Language notes

For more detailed notes, see the Business Grammar Guide.

Talking about the future

We can use several tenses to talk about the future. In some situations (e.g. talking about arrangements) more than one tense could be used with little or no change in meaning.

Present Simple

We use the present simple:
- for scheduled events, timetables and arrangements

e.g. **What time does the flight arrive?**
  We arrive in New York at 7am.

- with the verb *be* for personal plans

e.g. – **How long are you here for?**
  – **I'm here until the 17th.**

Present Continuous

We use the Present Continuous for personal plans and arrangements (a future time reference must either be stated or understood from the context).

e.g. **What are you doing this weekend?**
  I'm leaving on Saturday.

going to + infinitive

We use *going to*:
- for intentions, plans and decisions that have been made before the moment of speaking

e.g. **What are you going to do for your holiday this year?**
  Today I'm going to talk about our savings plans.
  I'm going to look for another job.

- for predictions based on present evidence

e.g **Profits are going to be very good this year.**
  The staff are not going to like the decision.

will + infinitive

We use will:
- for sudden decisions made at the moment of speaking

e.g. **I'll call you back in half an hour.**
  I'll send you an email with all the details.

- for arranged events (but not personal plans); this usage has quite a formal feel

e.g. **The meeting will start at 11am.**

- for confirming things

e.g. **So you'll contact me by the end of the week.**

- for promises

e.g. **I'll do it immediately.**   **I won't forget.**

- for predictions (especially with *think*, *expect*)

e.g. **I expect I'll be a bit late.**
  I don't think our sales figures will be very good this year.

- for offers

e.g. **I'll give you a lift to the station.**

Future Continuous (*will + be + -ing*)

We use the Future Continuous:
- for arrangements and schedules

e.g. **I'll be staying for three nights.**
  When will you be arriving?
  I'm afraid Mr Sanchez won't be coming to the meeting.

The Future Continuous tense – forms

Affirmative:

They will be waiting for you …   I will be looking for a new job …

Negative:

I'm afraid we won't be coming.   She won't be expecting your call.

Interrogative:

Will you be meeting each other in Vancouver?
Will they be travelling to Ipoh by car?

Short answers:

Yes, we will.   No, we won't.   Yes, they will.   No, they won't.

Useful phrases

I'm calling on behalf of Irene Braun.
She'll be visiting the States in July.
She'll be staying in Boston for six days.
She'd like to see you while she's there.
She would like to visit you during her stay.

When does your flight arrive?
When do you get to Kuala Lumpur?
How long will you be staying in Malaysia?

What's her flight number?
What's your departure time?
What are your flight details?

Will you be coming by taxi?
Yes, we will. Do you know how much it will cost?
No we won't. We're going to hire a car.

Tell the driver to take the Sumner Tunnel.
Take the first exit.
Follow the signs to Allston.
Turn left at the fourth set of lights.

This time next week, I'll be in Baltimore.
I'll see you in a week's time.

We look forward to meeting you.
I hope to meet you while you're here.

Are you leaving for Vancouver on Tuesday?
Yes, I'll try and catch a morning flight.
But I'm going to spend the weekend back in Boston.

UNIT 23 Abroad on business

1 Overview

Key dialogues

Listen to these conversations and answer the questions.

a What ticket does he want?
  Does the price charged include a special discount?
b Where does the dialogue take place?
  When do they have to be in Lille?
c What do the hire charges include?
  Who is going to pay?
d How does the first speaker cope with jet lag?
  What does the second speaker do?

Preparation

Come to the lesson prepared to talk about any interesting trips you have made in your own country or abroad.

Make a list of travel situations where you might need English, especially situations which have caused difficulty in the past.

Revise any common travel vocabulary which you need, e.g. to do with customs, lost luggage.

Look at the Language Reference section for this unit on page 104.

2 Reading

Advice on jet lag

1 Read the text. Is the advice in line with your experience?
  In groups/ pairs exchange advice on how you make travelling by plane, train or car easier and more enjoyable.

Flying between London and New York

Westbound

- Take the last flight of the day from London. This allows a reasonable day's work prior to departure.
- Stay awake during the flight, or just have a short nap.
- Avoid alcohol, tea and coffee, all of which interfere with sleep.
- Go to bed within three hours of arrival.
- Fatigue from the flight is usually enough to ensure that you sleep. You might wake early – often at around 4am or 5am local time. To counteract this, take a mild sleeping pill.
- If you do get up early, avoid arranging important meetings at the end of the day.

Eastbound

- Flights usually depart early in the evening between 6pm and 9pm.
- Local time on arrival is early morning.
- Eat a light meal before taking off.
- Ask the cabin crew not to disturb you.
- Get a good night's sleep during the flight: consider taking a mild sleeping pill as soon as you board the aircraft.
- If you are travelling from the east coast of the United States, take the smallest effective dose. Standard doses are based on a likely eight-hour night and you may arrive feeling drugged rather than refreshed.
- Once back in Britain, you might wake late in the morning and find it difficult to get to sleep at the normal time.

From *How to Stay Healthy Abroad*, by Richard Dawood

Refer to the Language Notes on page 104 as you complete these exercises.

when, as soon as, while, before, *etc. in future sentences*

1 Write these sentences in full.

e.g. I see her / give her your regards

(when) .....When I see her, I'll give her.....

.....your regards......

a I not sleep / get to New York
(until) ....

b be able to do it / you go?
(before) ....

c I get to my hotel / have a bath
(as soon as) ....

d you be working / you in France?
(while) ....

e let you know / they call the flight
(when) ....

f I call you / taxi here
(as soon as) ....

g Where you be staying / in Berlin?
(while) ....

Some travel vocabulary

2 Put the words into an appropriate group. Some words can go in more than one group.

▸ jet lag	▸ customs	▸ travel sickness
▸ transfer desk	▸ long-haul flight	▸ dual carriageway
▸ hydrofoil	▸ ferry terminal	▸ toll bridge
▸ duty free	▸ petrol station	▸ parking meter
▸ runway	▸ overbooking	▸ buffet car
▸ chauffeur	▸ level crossing	▸ security check

air ...*jet lag*.......................................

sea ...*travel sickness*..........................

land ...*dual carriageway*.....................

Now explore your particular areas of interest regarding travel vocabulary, e.g. air travel:

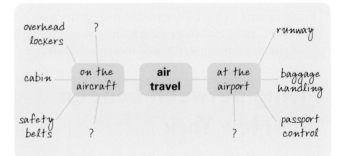

overhead lockers — ? — runway

cabin — on the aircraft — **air travel** — at the airport — baggage handling

safety belts — ? — ? — passport control

easy to/difficult to, *etc.*

3 In pairs, discuss how you cope with the following.

a Stress.
b Working while travelling.
c Sleeping on planes.
d Eating meals at irregular hours.

e.g. – It's easy to cope with stress.
  – Do you think so? I find it quite difficult.

  – I find it difficult to sleep on planes.
  – Do you? I don't. I just take a sleeping pill.

4 | Application

Some travel situations

1 Listen to the dialogues and answer the questions.

a A hotel check-in

   i Does the hotel have a single room with a bath?

   ii What does the $150 include?

   iii Where does Mr Vanta want the bill to be sent?

b A railway booking office

   iv When is the passenger travelling?

   v Why is it a good idea to reserve a seat?

   vi How does he want to pay?

c A car hire firm

   vii What kind of car is the customer looking for?

   viii What do the company's rates include?

   ix How long does she want the car?

2 In pairs, identify situations where you might hear these phrases. Some may be used in several situations. Practise the situations you meet most often.

a I have a reservation in the name of Bazri.

b A day return to Frankfurt, please.

c Can I check my bags through to Casablanca?

d They sell them in the gift shop.

e Turn right, then left, then right again.

f Have you got any euros?

g They're very nice. How much are they?

h I have to leave tomorrow morning before breakfast.

i Can you take the next turning on the left?

j It's a present for my daughter.

k Does that include insurance?

5 | Talking points

Transport delays

1 Read the advice for delayed passengers. Use a dictionary where necessary. Do you follow any of this advice? Have you had any experience of delayed flights? Talk about your experiences.

2 What advice would you give to a colleague who is stranded at an airport/railway station in your country?

THE DELAYED PASSENGER'S
Airport Survival Guide

→ Pack for an overnight stay.
→ If you don't, it will probably happen.
→ If you do, it might not.

Include

- Any medication to be taken regularly.
- Refresher wipes or sprays for cooling the face or feet.
- Small toilet bag with soap, toothbrush and paste, make-up or shaving equipment, contact lens cases and solutions, hand towel.
- Hand-held battery-operated fan.
- Traveller's pillow – the inflatable sort that fits round the neck.
- Plenty to read.
- Games such as travelling chess or cards.
- For children, take a selection of favourite toys and games, disposable nappies, etc.

Diversions

- Aircraft spotting.
- People-watching – probably the most fascinating exercise.
- Talk to someone you do not know – this may relieve the tedium of complaints and raised tempers within the family group.
- Learn a language, read your phrase book.
- Visit the place of worship. It may also be possible to spend some time just meditating.
- If you haven't gone into the Departure Lounge, go into the short-term car park for a walk. The dark and cool are surprisingly refreshing.
- Make a nuisance of yourself at any information desk which refuses to give you information.

From *The Times*

LANGUAGE REFERENCE

Language notes

For more detailed notes, see the Business Grammar Guide.

when, as soon as, while, before, etc.

Note how we use *when, as soon as, while, before*, etc. in future sentences.

e.g. Will you see John before he leaves?
Where will you be staying while you are here?
I won't sleep until I get to Berlin.
As soon as we hear from them, we'll let you know.
After you pass the station, you'll see a factory on your right.

Note that we use the Present tense form of the verb after these words.

easy/difficult to, etc.

Note these examples of adjectives followed by *to*.

e.g. The directions are easy to follow.
I find it difficult to drive on the left.
It's important to decide now.
It's not necessary to book a seat.
It's quite common to have delays.
It's quicker and cheaper to go by car.

Some more travel vocabulary

railway carriage	security screening
railway platform	emergency exit
ticket inspection	aisle seat
ticket machine	middle seat
ticket barrier	window seat
driving licence	motorway services
speed cameras	motorway junction
road works	congestion

Useful phrases

Do you find it difficult to sleep on long-haul flights?
No I don't. I can get to sleep anywhere at anytime!
Do you find it easy to cope with jet lag?
Is it difficult to stay awake?

I'll call you as soon as I arrive in Moscow.
I won't eat until I get to the hotel.
Will you have time to eat later?
Where will you be staying while you're there?

I've booked a four-star rather than a five-star hotel. Is that OK?
Would you rather go by train than fly?
I don't mind. Whichever is quickest.
We're meeting in the morning rather than in the afternoon.

Are there any delays on the motorway?
Yes, there are some road works about 20 kilometres ahead.
There have been some terrible traffic jams.
Thanks for the warning.

Do your hire rates include insurance?
Yes, they include everything except fuel.
So how much do I owe you?
€365 excluding tax.
Can you send the bill to my company?
Sure. Could you sign here, please?

UNIT 24 Returning from a business trip

1 Overview

Key dialogues

Listen to the exchanges and answer the questions.

a What was she doing in Brazil?
   What does she say about São Paulo?
b Where was the hotel exactly?
   How did they get there?
   What was his opinion of the hotel?
c Why is she writing her report today?
   Was it a worthwhile trip?

Preparation

Come to the lesson prepared to talk about countries or areas which you have visited. Consider: population, neighbouring countries, names of main regions/cities, etc.

Prepare to describe the accommodation you have stayed in.

Prepare to ask and answer questions needed to elicit information about a country or region such as: *'Where is it exactly?'*, *'Is it near …?'*, etc.

Refer to the unit Language Notes and Useful Phrases on page 108.

2 Practice

Back from Brazil

Work in pairs.

Partner A: Read the notes on Brazil and the covering letter. Then call **Partner B** for further details. Ask about:

- background information on Brazil
- more population figures
- further information on the size of the regions
- more information on the regions' main industries
- additional information on export possibilities
- a specific figure for GDP
- further details on Rio Grande do Sul.

Partner B: You wrote the notes. You have some more information on page 136.

Dear Mario

I enclose some notes on my recent trip to Brazil. Our agent in São Paulo was very helpful. I made some good contacts. Please get back to me if you need further details.

Yours

Alex

Brazil is the largest country in Latin America. It is a founder member of the Latin American Integration Association (ALADI – www.aladi.org). The country is divided into nine major economic areas, the wealthiest of which are São Paulo, Rio de Janeiro and Minas Gerais.

São Paulo

São Paulo is the same size as the United Kingdom and has the heaviest concentration of industrial firms in Latin America. It accounts for 55% of Brazil's industrial output and 43% of its GDP. It offers major opportunities for direct export and joint venture operations, particularly in the more advanced areas of technology.

Rio de Janeiro

Known as the 'gateway to Brazil', this is the second largest industrial centre in the region. It has a population of approximately 14 million, its main industries being offshore oil and gas, chemicals, petrochemicals, steel, cement and alcohol.

Minas Gerais

In terms of economic activity, this is the third most important state in Brazil. The main industries in Minas Gerais are mining, steel production and capital goods, and it offers major opportunities for export and technology transfer, particularly in the mining, metallurgy, food processing, biotechnology, chemicals and micro-electronics industries.

Other major trading areas are Espirito Santo (which has seen growth rates higher than the national average), Parana (the base for more than 170 manufacturing firms) and Rio Grande do Sul.

Refer to the Language Notes on page 108 as you do these exercises.

in case

1 Write *if* or *in case* in the gaps.

e.g. I'll wear my cold weather gear ....*if*.... it snows.
I'll take my cold weather gear,....*in case*.... it snows.

a I'll get to the airport by 12, ... the plane is early.

b .... the plane is early, they will have to wait for us.

c I'll write my report today, ... they need it tomorrow.

d .... I finish it before you go home, I'll let you have a copy.

e .... the airline lose my bags, I'll claim on the insurance.

f I'd better insure my bags, ... I lose them.

g I'll book a table for four, ... Petra comes.

h We'll need a table for four .... Petra comes.

Points of the compass

2 Make a note of five or six large towns or cities in your country and describe their locations in relation to the capital city. Refer the compass in the Language Notes.

e.g. Sundsvall is to the north-east of Stockholm. Bristol is about 180 kilometres west of London. Yerevan is 300 kilometres south of Tbilisi.

a long way, a long time

3 In pairs, practise asking about distances and times.

e.g. – How far is it to [Lima] from here?
  – It's a long way. It's about 1400 kilometres.
  – How long does it take to get there?
  – It depends on how you travel …

Ranking

4 Write sentences comparing the cities in this table.

	Population	Av. winter temp.	Av. summer temp.	Av. monthly rain
Buenos Aires	10.7m	10°	20°	70mm
Chicago	8.1m	0°	22°	50mm
Lima	4.6m	19°	22°	8mm
Los Angeles	13.1m	15°	18°	20mm
Rio de Janeiro	5.6m	20°	25°	100mm

e.g. Of the cities listed, Chicago is ....*the third*.... ....*largest*.... . (large)

a Buenos Aires is .... in summer. (cool)

b Los Angeles is .... in winter. (warm)

c Los Angeles is .... (dry)

d Buenos Aires is .... (wet)

e Rio de Janeiro has .... population. (small)

f Lima has .... winter temperature. (high)

g Buenos Aires ....

h Chicago ....

4 Listening

Back from a trip

1 Listen to an oil engineer talking about a recent visit to Nevtchugansk in Siberia. Did he enjoy his visit? Are these statements true ☐T☐ or false ☐F☐?

  a He went by train from Moscow. ☐

  b It was a comfortable trip. ☐

  c He spent about three days there. ☐

  d Nevtchugansk has a population of approximately 100,000. ☐

  e Chelyabinsk is north-east of Nevtchugansk. ☐

  f He took his cold weather clothes. ☐

2 In pairs or groups, report back on a trip you have made. Refer to the useful questions box to help you.

> **Useful questions**
>
> Where exactly is it?
> What is it like?
> Is it far from …?
> What's the population?
> What are the main industries?
> How did you get there?
> How long were you there?
> Where did you stay?

5 Application

Commenting on accommodation

In pairs, talk specifically about the accommodation you have had when you have been abroad/away from home. You might comment on the service you received, the cleanliness of the hotel, the standard of equipment in the room/bathroom, the quality of the food, special features of the hotel and overall value for money.

e.g. – Where did you stay when you were in France?

  – We stayed in an excellent hotel near Dax, which is in the south-west. It had by far the best restaurant I have ever eaten in …, etc.

LANGUAGE REFERENCE

Language notes

For more detailed notes, see the Business Grammar Guide.

in case

Note the following examples.

e.g. I sent the report in case he needed it today.
Ring me on Monday in case I have some news.
We'd better call them in case they're waiting.
I'll take a square one in case we run out.

Rankings

Note the following examples.

e.g. the third most important state in the region
the second largest company in the world
the fourth richest country in Latin America
the second most expensive city in Europe

Points of the compass

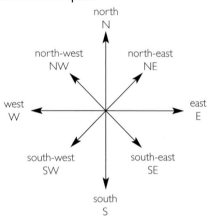

Useful phrases

I'm just back from a trip to Brazil.
I made some good contacts while I was there.
It's a fantastic country!

Brazil is the largest country in Latin America.
It's divided into nine economic areas.
It's one of the 20 richest countries worldwide.
It's a member of ALADI.
What does ALADI stand for?

Minas Gerais is the third most important state in the region.
        the second largest   the fourth richest
São Paulo accounts for 55% of the country's output.
It has a population of 33 million.
The main industries are mining and steel production.

How far is it to São Paulo from here?
Not far.   It's a long way.
How long does it take to get there?
Is it a long journey?

What were you doing in Salvador?
I was there on business.
How long were you there?
What was your hotel like?
Excellent. By far the best hotel I have ever stayed in.

I'll send the report today, in case they need it tomorrow.
If it arrives it before you go home, I'll let you have a copy.

UNIT 25 Personal finances

1 Overview

Key dialogues

Listen, then answer the questions.

a Is the speaker well-off in his opinion?
Do they spend much on holidays?

b What was stolen?
Are they insured?

c Does the speaker have an expensive car?
Does the speaker spend a lot of money?

d What does the figure of 2612 represent?
Is expenditure on telephone and postage up or down?

Preparation

Come to the lesson prepared to talk about how you and other people in your country typically spend personal income.

If possible, try to get hold of some statistics. It may be difficult to generalise nationally, but you may have thoughts about regional characteristics.

Refer to the Useful Phrases and Language Notes for this unit, which are on page 112.

2 Practice

Personal expenses

How do these rules from a UK company about personal expenses compare with those in your company, and/or other companies which you know.

When undertaking business on behalf of the company – for example, training or meetings which are not held on company premises – you are permitted the following personal expenditure, as long as receipts are provided.

1 Reasonable travel expenses.

2 If overnight accommodation is necessitated by training or a meeting and no free accommodation is available, then you may spend up to £75 per night on overnight accommodation. Such expenditure must be discussed in advance with Finance. If expenditure beyond this level is required, then prior approval must be sought from Finance.

3 If an overnight stay is required or travel to a meeting/training event begins before 7.30am, then you may claim up to £12 for breakfast.

4 If lunch is not provided as part of a meeting/training event, then provision for expenditure on lunch is allowed up to £20.

5 If an evening meal is not provided as part of a meeting/training event, then you may claim for an evening meal up to the value of £30.

6 If overnight accommodation is necessitated by training or a meeting and you stay with friends or family, then an evening meal allowance of up to £120 is allowed (so that you may take your host out for a meal).

7 If it is essential that you need to attend a meeting when you have childcare responsibilities, the company will provide payment for such childcare as required. All receipts should be forwarded to Finance as soon as possible so that costs can be reimbursed. Receipts should be accompanied by a petty cash authorisation form.

The Finance office must ratify any personal expenditure not covered by these clauses.

3 Listening

Everyday expenditure

1 Listen to the conversation. Then tick the items that the speaker spends money on. Note the speaker's use of *do* and *did* (we *do* spend money on our hobbies), used for emphasis. See the Language Notes on page 112.

charities	☐	eating out	☐	clothes	☐
holidays, foreign travel	☐	religious activities	☐	food and groceries	☐
theatre and other arts events	☐	children	☐	cars	☐
books	☐	antiques	☐	sport	☐

4 Language focus

Some insurance terms

1 Note the insurance terms in the Language Notes on page 112. Then read the text and answer the questions.

Marc and Sophie's story

Late last year, our home was broken into and our TV and computer were taken. We thought we would make some easy money by adding a few things to our insurance claim. Insurance companies don't check small claims, we thought – but they did, and we had no receipts. A week later, the police caught the thief and he admitted to stealing the television and computer, but nothing else. We were interviewed and found out. Insurance evidence helped with the prosecution. We were each fined £500 – an expensive lesson for us.

a What happened to Marc and Sophie at the end of last year?

b How did they think they would make some money?

c What happened to the thief a week later?

d Then what happened to Marc and Sophie?

2 In pairs, make a list of some valuable items – either at home or in the office. Practise the discussion which might follow the theft of those items.

e.g. – Someone broke into my …
   – Is there anything missing?
   – Yes, they took my …
   – Do you know what it's/they're worth?
   – I suppose it's/they're worth about …
   – Are you insured?
   – Yes, I'll have to make a claim.

Some financial vocabulary

3 Complete the sentences using these verbs in their correct forms.

► reimburse	► afford	► cash	► clear
► earn	► go ✔	► keep	► pay
► spend	► claim		

e.g. About 24% of my income *goes* in tax.

a Do you .... your savings in a high interest account?

b We .... most of our regular outgoings by direct debit.

c I suppose he .... about $57,000, with bonuses.

d I need to .... my overdraft. It's too high.

e They .... about $300 per month on food.

f We can't .... to run two cars.

g I need to .... a cheque.

h You need to keep your receipts so that we can .... you.

i I need to .... my travel expenses.

Fees and expenses

1 Sally Voight runs a small business in the UK. She is a self-employed media consultant. In pairs, complete this extract from her fees and expenses.

Partner A: Your information is below.
Partner B: Your information is on page 136.

> **Useful language**
>
> How much did she spend on [clothing]?
> What's the figure for [depreciation]?
> What's the figure of [£2,612] for?
> What does this figure represent?

2 Compare the current year with the year before. Compare the items of expenditure with your own. Refer to the examples of fractions and multiples on page 112.

e.g. She spent less/more on .... this year than last year.
I/We spend about half as much as this.

SALLY VOIGHT PRODUCTIONS LTD
FEES AND EXPENSES

	Current year (£)	Last year (£)
Turnover (fee income)	163,141	159,244
EXPENSES		
Secretarial assistant	15,000	
Wardrobe / clothing	....	4,477
Travelling, accommodation & subsistence	8,791	13,519
Lighting & heating	1,127	2,281
....	2,612	2,163
Telephone & postage	1,501	3,446
Professional books, journals & subscriptions	....	1,229
Entertainment	2,566	2,620
Photography	....	352
Company registration expenses	25	40
Company pension plan	36,167	....
Director's remuneration	80,604	97,198
Depreciation	....	300
....	3,100	2,200
Sundry expenses	316	994
Insurance	989	....
Cleaning	920	760
Theatre visits & research expenses	340	105

LANGUAGE REFERENCE

Language Notes

For more detailed notes, see the Business Grammar Guide.

do and *did* emphasis

We use *do/did* for emphasis and to correct misunderstandings. Note the following examples.

e.g. He does have the account number.
We did send you the tax form.
I did enjoy your talk.
We do spend money on hobbies, but not much.
We did go away for a week last year, but that was exceptional.

Some insurance terms

Note the following examples.

e.g. Are you insured?
The premium was paid on the last day of January.
Are you covered for theft?
Can you arrange for [immediate cover]?
We need to renew our policy.
We'll have to make a claim.
Could you send me a claim form?
You can be fined if you make a false claim.

Fractions and multiples: some examples

Fractions:

She earns half as much as he does.
She earns half of what he does.
We normally spend a quarter of that.
We spend a fraction of that on …

Multiples:

They spend twice as much on housing as we do.
Their taxes are double what we pay.
Their advertising budget is three times the size of ours.
We pay five times more than they do.

Useful phrases

We spend a lot of money on groceries.
We spend very little on holidays.
We did go abroad for a week last year, but that was unusual.

I'm trying to save up for a holiday.
But I do still spend a lot of money on my hobbies.
About 24% of my income goes in tax.
I pay most of my bills by direct debit.
I can just afford to run two cars.
But I do need to clear my overdraft.

Have you claimed your travel expenses yet?
Not yet. What can you claim for?
The company will pay for dinner and overnight accommodation.
All travel expenses are reimbursed.

Have you seen the figures?
How much did you spend on eating last year?
Expenditure was up.
Expenditure was similar to last year.

I normally spend about half as much as she spends on books.
… twice as much as she spends.
… far more than she spends.

Our house was broken into last night.
The thieves took the TV.
It's worth about $500.
Are you insured?
Yes, I'll have to make a claim on my insurance (policy).

UNIT 26 Company finances

1 | Overview

Key dialogues

Listen and answer the questions.

a By how much did revenue increase
last year?
Why are profits disappointing?

b How are they responding to the
competition?
When will they see the benefits of
the reorganisation?

c What's the value of their fixed
assets?
How much do they owe?

d What's the value of the company?
Has it been a good year?

Preparation

Bring to the lesson a recent financial report, set of
accounts, or other financial information about your
company or one which is of interest to you.

You may wish to focus on the everyday financial
language and grammar points in this unit if you have a
low level of interest or knowledge of company
finances.

Refer to the Useful Phrases and Language Notes for
this unit, which are on page 116.

2 | Reading

The balance sheet

1 Read the text and then select words in the box to
match the definitions.

> ► stakeholders/investors ► past profits ► current assets
> ► loans ► deferred taxation ► fixed assets
> ► creditors ► debtors ► benefits

a What we need to run a company-buildings, plant,
motor vehicles, etc. ....

b People or organisations, that you owe money to.
....

c People who buy shares on the stock exchange.
....

d What we need to trade – e.g. our stocks.
....

e People or organisations that owe us money.
....

f Tax to be paid in the future. ....

The balance sheet

The balance sheet of a company is a statement of what
it owns (assets) and what it owes (liabilities) at a
particular time – usually the last day of the company's
financial year. It is composed of three major classes of
item: assets, liabilities and owners' equity.

Assets are resources of the company that have the
potential for providing it with future economic services
or benefits. Assets must be split into fixed assets (such as
land, buildings, plant vehicles and intangible assets
such as goodwill) and current assets (such as stocks of
raw materials, work-in-progress and finished goods,
debtors, short-term investments, prepaid expenses and
cash).

Liabilities include obligations of a company to make
payment in the foreseeable future for goods or services
already received. Statute requires a company to
distinguish between creditors who require payment
within one year and those due after more than one year.
Other liabilities include long-term debt, comprising
loans and obligations under long-term leases, and
deferred tax (provisions for tax payable or recoverable
in future where the tax effect of a transaction is
recognised in a different period to the accounting
effect).

From *The Manager's Handbook*, Ernst & Young

Refer to the Language Notes on page 116 as you complete these exercises.

The Passive

1 Make these questions passive. Then supply possible answers.

e.g. When did you complete the accounts?

When were the accounts completed?

They were completed last week.

a Have you set targets for the coming year?

....

b When will you announce the new prices?

....

c Did they approve the accounts of the AGM?

....

d How can you measure management performance?

....

e How much does the company owe?

....

f Have you transferred the funds yet?

....

g Where are they going to locate the new plant?

....

2 Rewrite this statement using Passive forms where possible. Write a similar statement about your company.

> The value of the company is currently about $20 million. Last year, we set tough financial targets, which we met without difficulty. In the accounting period to the end of December, we increased profits by more than 15%. We announced these results in January, and the AGM approved the accounts in March. We have established equivalent targets for the current year.

Common business abbreviations

3 What do the following abbreviations stand for? What others do you know? Work in pairs. Then check the answers and Language Notes.

a	VAT	**c**	AGM	**e**	IOU	**g**	RPI	**i**	o/s
b	a/c	**d**	b/f	**f**	PTO	**h**	bal	**j**	GDP

An annual review of a company

1 Listen to the presentation by the chairman of an airport authority, based on an annual review. Number the points in the order they are made.

Catering revenue per passenger increased by 5.7% over last year. ☐

In the year to the end of March, productivity increased by 6.5%. ☐

Retail expansion will continue with the opening of 90 new shops. ☐

In November, the Aviation Authority announced its new pricing formula. ☐1

Staff numbers were reduced and the quality of the service improved. ☐

The new pricing formula sets tough targets for the coming period. ☐

A key factor in these results is the quality of the management team. ☐

The Authority increased overall revenue by expanding airport retailing. ☐

2 Say something about the key factors that have influenced your business in recent years.

5 | Application
Comparing company performance

1 Work with a partner. Find out the recent financial performance of his/her company or another company of interest.

Profit and loss

What was your turnover/revenue in .... ?
What were your total sales?
How much profit was made?
What was the dividend last year?

Overall revenue increased by .... over the period ....
Gross profit rose by ....
Domestic sales accounted for .... of our total revenue.

Balance sheet

What is the value of your fixed assets?
... and of your current assets/liabilities?
How much is owed?
What is the total value of the company?

Net assets are in the region of ....
Gross liabilities are just over ....
The company is valued at between .... and ....

2 Summarise what you have found out.
   e.g. It was a good year for Kolova Steel.
   Profits were up compared with the previous year by 3%.
   The company increased its dividend to shareholders.
   The only disappointment was domestic sales, which were down on the previous year.

LANGUAGE REFERENCE

Language notes

For more detailed notes, see the Business Grammar Guide.

The Passive

The passive is formed with the verb *to be* + past participle:

Affirmative:

The accounts	**are**	**filed**	in June.
The flight	**has been**	**cancelled.**	
The company	**was**	**founded**	in 1909.
The goods	**should be**	**delivered**	tomorrow.

Negative:

| The meeting | **is not going to be held** | in this room. |
| We | **weren't** | **invited** | to the talk. |

Questions:

	Has	the invoice	been	**sent?**
When	**will**	the decision	**be**	**announced?**
Why	**was**	the meeting	**postponed?**

- The passive is always used for a reason. It is not simply another way of saying the active form. We use the passive when we do not know or are not interested in the person or thing which performs the action (the agent).
  e.g. The figures **are checked** very carefully. (We are not interested in who checks them.)

Some business abbreviations

attn	=	for the attention of
cc	=	copies to
co	=	company
dept	=	department
encl	=	enclosed
ext	=	extension (number)
ICT	=	Information and Communication Technology
HO	=	headquarters
HR	=	Human Resources
PA	=	personal assistant
PIN	=	personal identity number
PLC	=	public limited company
PR	=	public relations
re	=	regarding, in connection with
ref	=	reference

Useful phrases

The company has just announced its results.
The balance sheet for this year is very healthy.
The accounts were approved at the AGM.

What's the value of your fixed assets?
What are your current liabilities?
How much do you owe?
What's the total value of the company?

Net assets are in the region of £40 million.
Gross liabilities are just over £10 million.
The company is valued at between $20 and $30 million.

A key factor in these results is the quality of our management team.
Our number one aim is to satisfy our customers' needs profitably.

What was your turnover in that period?
What were your total sales?
How much profit did you make?
What was the dividend last year?

Productivity increased by 6.5%.
The quality of our service improved.
Overall revenue increased by 5.7% over the first quarter.
Domestic sales accounted for 33% of our total revenue.

This was achieved by offering excellent value for money.
… better service   … greater choice
Tough targets have been set for the coming year.

UNIT 27 Payment issues

Preparation

If appropriate, be prepared to describe how customers usually pay your company, or how your company pays its suppliers. Explain the stages involved in making payments, including items like order number, delivery note, invoice, transfer, statement, reminders, etc.

If you have no experience of making or receiving company payments, you may prefer to describe similar details concerning domestic bills.

Look at the Language Reference section for this unit on page 120.

1 Overview

Key dialogues

Listen to the dialogues and answer the questions.

a Why is she calling?
Has the invoice been paid?

b What are the invoice details?
Have the goods been delivered?

c Is there a problem with this invoice?

When can the caller expect payment?

d Why haven't they paid?
What is the supplier going to do?

2 Practice

A request for payment

1 Read the email. In your opinion, is this a first, second or third reminder?

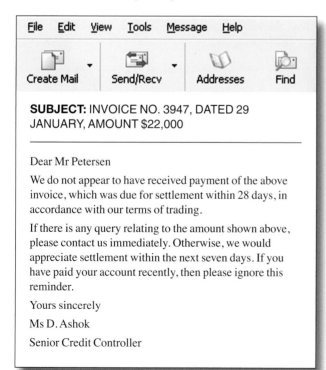

File Edit View Tools Message Help

Create Mail   Send/Recv   Addresses   Find

SUBJECT: INVOICE NO. 3947, DATED 29 JANUARY, AMOUNT $22,000

Dear Mr Petersen

We do not appear to have received payment of the above invoice, which was due for settlement within 28 days, in accordance with our terms of trading.

If there is any query relating to the amount shown above, please contact us immediately. Otherwise, we would appreciate settlement within the next seven days. If you have paid your account recently, then please ignore this reminder.

Yours sincerely

Ms D. Ashok

Senior Credit Controller

2 Write a reply in which you point out that you have paid the invoice. There is a sample on page 137.

3 Work in pairs.

Partner A (Ms Ashok): You have received a reply to your reminder. You have not received notification from the bank that Mr Petersen has paid. Phone **Partner B** (Mr Petersen) to resolve the issue.

Useful language

to pay by bank transfer
to transfer the money
to pay late
to lose the paperwork
I'll check (with the bank).
I'll sort it out.
I'll get back to you.

3 Language focus

Check the Language Notes on page 120 as you do these exercises.

unless *and* providing/provided

1 Complete the sentences using *unless* or *providing/provided*.

   a We will take no further action .... we receive payment within seven days.

   b I'll lend you the money .... you repay me tomorrow.

   c They never pay .... you remind them.

   d You can use my office .... you don't smoke.

   e I'll assume everything is OK .... I hear from you.

   f I can't give you a cheque .... payment is approved.

   g Driving to work saves time .... you can find parking.

   h I'm going to leave .... I get a salary increase.

Prepositions related to payment

2 Complete the sentences.

   a Can we pay .... cheque?

   b We'd prefer to be paid .... cash.

   c Interest rates .... the loan are quite high.

   d We're overdrawn .... the bank.

   e I don't understand one of the entries .... my bank statement.

   f What is the rate of the yen .... the dollar?

   g Turnover has increased .... 15%.

   h I think they are .... debt.

Numbers and calculations

3 How would you say the following? Write the numbers/terms as you would say them.

   e.g. Let's split the cost (50-50) ..... *fifty fifty.*

   a It'll cost between ($300–$500) ....

   b What is (5000 ÷ 325) .... ?

   c What is (5.3 × 8.7) .... ?

   d (490,000) .... Korean Won.

   e What is (5.004 – 4.346) .... ?

   f ($^2/_5$) .... of our production is exported.

   g (5,600) .... Argentinian Pesos.

   h The tank has a capacity of (60m^3) ....

   i The plant covers an area of (500m^2) ....

4 Listening

Reasons for not paying

1 What are the most common and most unusual excuses for not paying bills?

2 Listen, then match the speakers with the reasons for not paying.

   a An Austrian financial controller

   b A New Zealand director of a real estate company

   c An English production manager for a publishing firm

   d A Scottish accountant

   e An Irish export manager

   i There is a query on the sum of money charged.

   ii Payment was, in fact, made as promised.

   iii The invoice was not addressed correctly.

   iv The invoice has possibly got lost in the internal mail.

   v The person who is authorised to make payments is away on business.

Invoice details

1 Listen to the phone call between VX Training Manuals and Festro Management Systems. Complete the invoice details.

INVOICE   VX TRAINING MANUALS

CHARGE TO:

DESPATCH TO:

DATE OF INVOICE: ...15 June......

INVOICE NUMBER: ....

DATE PAYABLE: ....

ORDER REF.	QUANTITY	SBN	TITLE	PRICE
FES/CLE/POS7/6	....	39832688	....	....
FES/CLE/POS7/6	....	39833788	....	....

DISCOUNT TERMS: ....   TOTAL PRICE: ....

2 Work in pairs. Use the invoice above as a template and agree details for another invoice issued by MT Training Manuals.

Partner A: You are the customer. Call **Partner B** to explain why the invoice has not been paid. Use the phrases below to help you.

> **Useful phrases**
>
> I'm calling in connection with your invoice of …
> It seems that it was passed for payment on …
> Your cheque should be in the next computer run.
> According to our records, it was paid .... ago.
> There was a query on this.
> Apparently, the invoice details didn't tie up with our records.
> I can't settle it unless payment is authorised.
> Didn't you get our letter?

Partner B: You work for MT Training Manuals. Your useful phrases are on page 137.

3 How often do you have problems with unpaid/late invoices? Are you a prompt or a late payer?

LANGUAGE REFERENCE

Language notes

For more detailed notes, see the Business Grammar Guide.

unless and *providing/provided*

Note the following examples.

e.g. We will take no further action provided we receive payment within the next 14 days.
He's arriving at 8.30 unless there's a delay.
Unless I hear from you, I'll assume everything is OK.

Numbers and mathematical terms.

Note these terms

÷	divided by
×	multiplied by/times
+	plus
−	minus
m^3	cubic metres
m^2	square metres
$^1/_4$	a quarter
$^1/_2$	a half
$^3/_4$	three-quarters
$^4/_5$	four-fifths
$^7/_8$	seven-eights

(See Units 4 and 10 for more on numbers.)

Some prepositions

to pay by cheque/bank transfer
to pay in cash
to be overdrawn at the bank
to check the rate of the Korean Won against the dollar
to be in credit/debit
to increase prices by 10%
to pay interest on a loan
to check something with the accounts department

apparently, *it seems that*, etc.

Note the following examples.

e.g. Apparently, there was a query on this.
We don't appear to have received it.
You seem to have paid twice.
It appears that they sent the payment last week.
It seems that it was passed for payment on the 10th.

Useful phrases

I'm calling about our invoice of May 27th.
It's about an unpaid invoice.
Can we pay you by cheque?
… by BACS?
We'd prefer to be paid in cash.

We don't appear to have received your payment.
The invoice is still outstanding.
It was due for payment on the 26th.
I'm sorry, but we have no record of your invoice.
Could you give me the details?
What was the invoice number?
What was the invoice for?   And the payment date?

It was for 25 training manuals at 25 pesos each.
The invoice value was 5000 pesos plus tax.

It seems that it was passed for payment on the 10th.
According to our records, it was paid two weeks ago.

We haven't settled the bill as we haven't received the goods.
Apparently, there was a query on the invoice.
That's why we haven't paid it yet.
Didn't you receive my message last week?

When can we expect payment?
Leave it with me. I'll sort it out.
I'll deal with it.
I'll arrange for the bank transfer immediately.
Our next cheque run is on Friday.

We'll take no further action providing we receive payment within 14 days.
I'll assume everything is OK unless I hear from you.

UNIT 28 Preparing for a presentation

1 Overview

Key dialogues

Listen to the conversations and answer the questions.

a Does Sergei have much experience of giving presentations?
What equipment does he need?

b What is she doing?
Has she got everything she needs?

c Is the woman good at giving presentations?
Is she used to presenting to large groups?

d Is he ready to start?
Is he going to be introduced?

> **Preparation**
>
> Be prepared to talk about the types of presentations which you have to give, from formal presentations to large audiences, to short informal presentations to small groups of colleagues/customers, etc.
>
> What are your experiences of explaining things in English to colleagues and business contacts?
>
> Refer to the unit Language Notes and Useful Phrases on page 124.

2 Practice

Tips on improving presentation skills

In pairs, discuss which of the following points are most important. Are there any points you disagree with? Are there any points you would add?

- ☐ **Plan your presentation.** Define your objective, research your audience, note down ideas and outline the structure of your talk.

- ☐ **Map out a route to help the audience follow your presentation.** Tell them where they are going, how they are going to get there and what the end result will be.

- ☐ **Visual aids** should be simple, striking and colourful. Pause to give your audience time to take them in.

- ☐ **Use humour** – but ensure it is appropriate to a business setting.

- ☐ **Rehearse to check timings and eliminate problems.** Plan introductions, handovers, seating arrangements and the position of any audio-visual equipment.

- ☐ **Watch your body language.** Stand squarely, use whole-arm gestures and don't fiddle with pens, jewellery or clothing – it will distract your audience and shows that you're nervous.

- ☐ **Be aware of your voice.** Control your breathing, slow down and speak clearly, and vary your volume and pitch.

- ☐ **Identify** and plan your responses in advance. Keep your answers brief.

- ☐ **Finish with a flourish.** Summarise your presentation and add a touch of light relief at the end.

Adapted from the *Evening Standard*

3 Language focus

Refer to the Language Notes on page 124 as you do these exercises.

Verb + preposition + -ing

1 Complete the sentences with the correct preposition.

a I look forward .... meeting you again soon.

b Thank you all .... coming.

c I must apologise .... starting a little late.

d She's thinking .... leaving the company.

e He's very good .... handling questions.

f Are you interested .... making some money?

g We specialise .... installing fire prevention equipment.

h I need to concentrate .... this?

Likes and dislikes

2 Complete the sentences, using the verbs in the box to help you if necessary.

▶ answer	▶ do	▶ give	▶ have	▶ listen
▶ live	▶ play	▶ speak	▶ work	▶ write

e.g. I'm (not) very keen on
...... *speaking to large audiences* ....

I much prefer ...... *doing business face to face to doing it on the phone* ....

a I don't mind ....

b I (don't) enjoy ....

c I'm fed up with ....

d I can't stand ....

e I'm very fond of ....

f I (absolutely) hate ....

g I love ....

h I sometimes don't feel like ....

to be used to and to get used to

3 Practise *to be/get used to* by writing sentences based on your experience. Then compare notes with a partner. Here are some examples.

I'm (not) used to	speaking to large groups.
I can't get used to	presenting in English.
I'll have to get used to	working at weekends.
	using new technology.
	living in this town.
	wearing glasses, etc.

e.g. I'm not used to speaking without notes.
I've got used to driving long distances in my current job.

4 Listening

Checking equipment

Listen to the telephone call. Tick ☑ the items the organiser will provide for the speaker's forthcoming presentation.

a flipchart ☐	an extension lead ☐
a network connection ☐	a tripod ☐
a screen ☐	a whiteboard ☐
a video player ☐	a DVD player ☐
a camera ☐	a digital projector ☐

5 Application

Final preparations

In pairs, practise preparing for a presentation.

Partner A: You are giving the presentation.
Partner B: You are the training manager. Does **Partner A** have everything he/she needs?

1 Set up the room for the presentation.

> **Useful language**
>
> How does the [projector] work?
> How do you switch it on?
> How do you adjust it?
> Could you get hold of an extension lead for me?
> I'll need some more [handouts].
> Do you have the [right connections]?
> Have you got everything you need?
> Are you planning to use [the projector]?
> The [bulb] needs changing – I'll get a new one.
> Is there a [network connection]?

2 Still in pairs, check that everything is ready.

> **Useful language**
>
> Is there anything else you need?
> Would you like a glass of water?
> How are you feeling?
> I'm not used to speaking without notes.
> We'll begin in five minutes if you're ready.
> Shall I introduce you?
> Good luck. I hope it goes well.

LANGUAGE REFERENCE

Language notes

For more detailed notes, see the Business Grammar Guide.

be used to and get used to

Affirmative:
We are used to working late.
You will soon get used to the travelling.

Negative:
I'm not used to using this equipment.
I'll never get used to these machines.

Interrogative:
Are you used to speaking in public?
Will they get used to the new system?

Short answers:

Yes, I am.	No, I'm not.
Yes, they will.	No, they won't.

Examples:
How quickly did you get used to not having a secretary?
I can't get used to working nights.
We're not used to such a long lunch break.
She's used to handling complaints from customers!

Verb + preposition + -ing

Examples:
to look forward to doing something
to apologise for arriving late
to be interested in changing career
to be for/against postponing the meeting
to specialise in building bridges
to concentrate on finding a new supplier
to thank someone for helping
to be good/bad at making decisions

Likes and dislikes

Examples:
I don't mind waiting.
I enjoy travelling.
I don't like rushing.
I hate queueing.

Useful phrases

I'm calling to check what equipment you need.
Are you planning to use a projector?
Do you mind using an ordinary whiteboard?

Is there a network connection?
I'll need a flipchart.
I'm used to working in all kinds of situations.

Is there anything else you need?
If I think of anything, I'll call you.
I look forward to meeting you next week.

How does the projector work?
How do you adjust it?
I'm afraid the bulb needs changing.
Could you get hold of an extension lead for me? Thank you.

Would you like me to introduce you?
Would you like a glass of water?
We'll begin in five minutes' time, if you're ready.

I'm not very keen on speaking to large audiences.
I can't get used to speaking in public.
I suppose I'll have to get used to it.
I'm used to speaking without notes.
I'm quite good at handling difficult questions.

Good morning everyone.
My name's Neil White and today I'd like to talk about …

UNIT 29 Presenting facts and figures

Preparation

Bring to the lesson graphic information (graphs, charts, tables, diagrams) relating to your company or relating to an interest of yours.

Be prepared to present and answer questions about a range of facts and figures.

Refer to the Language Notes and Language Summary on page 128.

1 | Overview

Key dialogues

Listen and answer the questions.

a What does the horizontal axis show?
Which line represents skilled workers?
b Which segment of the chart shows sales of childrenswear?
What does RST stand for?
c Are sales up compared with previous years?
What is the average value of each sale?
d How many stores do they have now?
Where does it refer to sales of salmon sandwiches?

2 | Practice

Describing a graph

1 Talk about trends and results related to your work, using adjectives and adverbs from the box below.

e.g. There was a *great* improvement in overall performance last year.
Overall, performance *greatly* improved last year.

There has been a *slight* rise in sales.
Sales have risen *slightly*.

▶ great/greatly	▶ slight/slightly
▶ fast/faster	▶ slow/slowly
▶ dramatic/dramatically	▶ gradual/gradually
▶ sudden/suddenly	▶ steady/steadily
▶ sharp/sharply	▶ significant/significantly

2 Present a graph, table or diagram which you have brought to the lesson to the rest of the group. The language in the box may help you.

Useful language

The horizontal axis shows …
[Sales figures] are shown on the vertical axis.
[Production levels] reached a peak in …
At this point on the curve …
There was a dramatic rise in …
In [2…] turnover fell sharply.
In [2…] there was a sudden fall in …
[Production figures] remained steady during …

Historical trends

1 The graph shows unemployment trends in Britain between 1975 and 1991. Listen to the recording and label the curves a, b and c that are not identified.

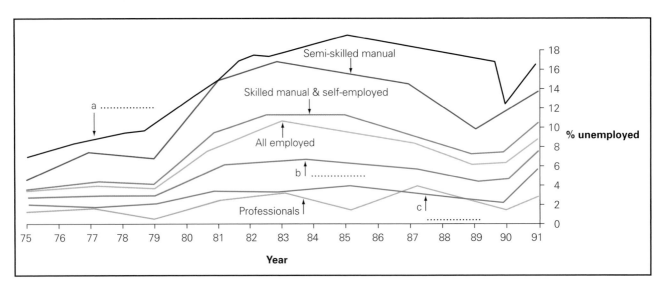

2 Complete the sentences using information in the graph.

e.g. The graph shows ......*the percentage of*........ ......*unemployed workers*........ in Britain between 1975 and 1991.

a In 1991, the overall rate of unemployment was ....

b The level of unemployment among unskilled manual workers rose sharply in ....

c The rate of unemployed for professionals peaked at .... in 1987.

d Among .... , unemployment rose to over 10% in 1983.

4 | Language focus

Refer to the Language Notes on page 128 as you complete these exercises.

Numerical information

1   In pairs, prepare as many statistics as you can, using the following phrases. Compare your examples with others in the group.

   a one in three/four
   b six/seven out of ten
   c every 20 seconds/minutes
   d every third car/lorry
   e between 15 and 20
   f three times as much/many … as
   g twice as much/many … as
   h half the quantity/number

   e.g. Every third car I see is a Toyota.
          We use three times as much recycled paper as we did five years ago.

Verb + infinitive or -ing

2   Compare the sentence below. Is there a change of meaning when the infinitive is changed to the gerund or vice versa?

   a Only one in three of our workers likes doing overtime.
          Only one in three of our workers likes to do overtime.
   b Every 20 seconds, somebody stops to smoke.
          Every twenty seconds, somebody stops smoking.
   c We saw him giving the presentation.
          We saw him give the presentation.
   d We began working on this project five years ago.
          We began to work on this project five years ago.
   e I don't remember saying that.
          I didn't remember to say that.

5 | Application

Locating information

1   Take it in turns to present information on a slide to the group. Members of the group ask questions.

   e.g. – This table shows .... The figures on the left-hand column are ....
          – Excuse me, what does the RFT stand for?
          – Where is that?
          – In the top left-hand corner, just below [the pie chart].

Useful language

in the top left-hand corner
in the bottom right-hand corner
at the top/bottom of the slide
on the right-hand slide
in the left-hand column
the second line from the top
the third bullet point
the first sentence
the final paragraph
the blue segment in the pie chart

Updating information

2   Work in pairs. Refer to the Language Notes on page 128.

   Partner A: The information you have below is now out-of-date. Contact **Partner B**, who has more recent facts and figures.

   Partner B: Your information is on page 137.

- There are 291 OIB stores in the country.
- OIB is the best-selling own label brand in the country.
- Sales average $517 per square foot.
- The flagship branch in Jojoba sells more specialist products per square foot than any other shop in the country.
- It makes a sale every 3.5 seconds.
- This store hands back more money in refunds than the average OIB branch takes.
- It is visited every day by 100,000 people – the capacity of a major stadium.
- It takes delivery of half a million items every week and has a delivery van of food or textiles arriving every five minutes.
- It sells 5500 sandwiches a day.
- It sells a ton of fresh and smoked salmon a week.

OIB is a fictitious company.

LANGUAGE REFERENCE

Language Notes

For more detailed notes, see the Business Grammar Guide.

Numerical information

See notes in Units 4, 10, 24 and 25.

Verbs followed by *-ing* or the infinitive

Some verbs are followed by the infinitive with *to* (e.g. *expect*, *hope*).

e.g. I want to see the figures first.

Some verbs are followed by the infinitive without *to* (e.g. *let*, *make*).

e.g. Do they make you work on Saturdays?

Some verbs are followed by *-ing* (e.g. *enjoy*, *dislike*, *practise*).

e.g. Do you enjoy travelling on business?

Some verbs can be followed by either the infinitive with *to* or *-ing*; the meaning does not change significantly. Note, for instance, *hate*, *like*, *love*, *prefer*, *begin*, *start*, *continue*, *intend*.

e.g. She likes working.
     She likes to work.

Some verbs can be followed by either the infinitive without *to* or *-ing*; the meaning does not change significantly. Note, for instance, *hear*, *notice*, *see*, *listen*, *watch*, *feel*.

e.g. We heard him come in.
     We heard him coming in.

Some verbs can be followed by either the infinitive or *-ing*, and the meaning changes. Note, for instance, *stop*, *remember*, *try*.

e.g. I tried to use more visual aids.
     I tried using more visual aids.

Updating information

Note the following phrases.

e.g. That (figure) has risen/fallen a lot/little/bit.
     It has gone up/down a lot/little/bit.

The number of deliveries is about the same as last year.
The sales figure hasn't changed at all.
Income hasn't changed much.

Average

As an adjective:
The average hotel stay is 1.8 nights.
The figures in the left-hand column are average sales per branch.

As a verb:
The first five months averaged an increase of 8% per month.
We average 6000 units per month.

Useful phrases

These figures are based on a survey of around 19,000 people.
The graph shows unemployment trends.
This line shows the rate of unemployment.
The year is shown here.

As you can see, the overall rate was just under 9%.
At this point on the curve, there is a sharp fall.
The level of unemployment falls sharply here.
... rises gradually   ... remains constant

Here the figure goes down dramatically.
And here it rises slightly.
The sales figures haven't changed at all.
The figure for calls per day is about the same as it was last year.

The figures in the left-hand column represent average sales per branch.
... in the top right-hand corner
... at the bottom of the page
... in the final sentence
... mentioned in the third bullet point

Sales average $517 per square foot.
On average, we make a sale every 3.5 seconds.
We now sell twice as much as we did two years ago.
We now employ half the number of staff.
But only one in three of our staff is prepared to work overtime.

I didn't remember to bring last year's figures with me.
I don't remember sending them.
I must remember to send them next time!

UNIT 30 Delivering a presentation

1 Overview

Key dialogues

Listen, then answer the questions.

a How is he organising his talk? What does the table show?

b What does the speaker want to talk about? Is the audience familiar with terms like 'Lord' and 'Sir'?

c Is there time for more questions? What did Monica say earlier?

d How successful was the presentation? What would the speaker like to change next time?

Preparation

In this unit, you will be asked to make a presentation on a subject of your choice. Come prepared with charts, graphs, diagrams, etc.

Refer to the Useful Phrases and Language Notes for this unit, which are on page 132.

2 Practice

Phrases used in presentations

Note some phrases which will be useful when you give presentations. In pairs, add other phrases to the lists.

Introducing the subject
I'm going to talk about …
The title of today's presentation is …
This talk is about …

Signposting the talk
First (of all), I'll tell you a bit about …
First, I'll give you a brief overview of …
Then I'll say a few words about …
And finally …

Referring to a point
Regarding …   With regard to …
Concerning …   With reference to …

Referring forward
I'll say (a bit) more about that in a moment.
I'll come back to that later on.

Referring back
As I said/mentioned earlier/before …
Going back to what I said earlier …

Moving on
That brings me (on) to my next point.
Let's move on to the question of …

Asking for clarification
Can I ask a question?
Could you just say a little more about …?
What exactly do/did you mean by …?

Referring to visuals
As you can see from this diagram …
These figures show …
If we look at this chart …

Giving examples
For instance …   For example …
Let me give you an example …

Problems
Can everyone see that OK?
It's not in focus.   It's out of focus.
Can you hear me at the back?

Inviting questions
Any questions so far?
Does everyone follow that?
Is that clear?
Does anyone/everyone know what … is?

Finishing off
I'd like to hand over to [Yanwen Liu] now.
Well, that was a brief overview of …
I hope that's given you some idea of …
Does anyone have any questions?

3 | Language focus

Refer to the Language Notes on page 132 as you complete these exercises.

because, as, since, so *and* therefore

1 Combine the sentences.

> **a** We are running late.
> **b** There is no employment in this area.
> **c** There was a plane strike.
> **d** He doesn't understand English.
> **e** The conference room is occupied at that time.

> **i** We had to come by train.
> **ii** We need an interpreter.
> **iii** The talk will take place in the boardroom.
> **iv** There is no time for more questions.
> **v** Many people are moving abroad.

a (as) *As we are running late, there is no time for more questions.*

(because) ....

b (since) ....
(therefore) ....

c (so) ....
(as) ....

d (since) ....
(so) ....

e (because) ....
(therefore) ....

although, even though, in spite of

2 Change the sentences.

e.g. In spite of the fact that she prepared carefully, her presentation didn't go well.

(although) *Although she prepared carefully her presentation didn't go well.*

a Although it was brand new, the camera didn't work.
(in spite of) ....

b We were on time, in spite of the terrible traffic.
(even though) ....

c He didn't get the job, in spite of having excellent qualifications.
(but) ....

d I work for the company, but I don't buy their products.
(although) ....

e Nobody placed an order, even though the presentation was excellent.
(in spite of) ....

f In spite of the fact he is nearly 80, he works seven hours a day.
(even though) ....

g Although he isn't very good at giving demonstrations, he gets excellent sales.
(in spite of) ....

Working in pairs, use *although*, *even though* and *in spite of* in short exchanges like this.

e.g. – How did it go?
  – Not very well, even though she had prepared carefully.

  – How was the reception?
  – It was very successful in spite of the fact it rained all day.

  – How was the journey?
  etc.

4 | Listening

Presenting information

Listen to two people presenting information on a company called Oknover. Compare the presentations and answer the questions below, putting ☐1 for the first speaker and ☐2 for the second speaker. In your opinion …

a … which presentation is by the finance director of a rival company? ☐

b … which one is by the PR manager of Oknover? ☐

c … which one is made to a board meeting? ☐

d … which one is made to journalists? ☐

e … which one is clearer? ☐

f … which one is more interesting? ☐

5 | Application

Giving a presentation

Prepare a brief presentation on a subject of your choice. As you prepare, keep in mind some of the following points. Try to use some of the phrases discussed in **2 Practice**. Deliver your presentation to the group.

- Focus on your interaction with the audience.
- Speak clearly.
- Project your enthusiasm.
- Allow time for questions.
- Keep questions under control and focused on the subject.
- Relax.
- Look around the room and at different parts of the audience.
- Find your own position of comfort with weight evenly balanced.
- Don't let the audience take control.
- Don't be too casual in your approach.
- Don't get irritated if someone heckles you.
- Don't use jargon – the audience might not be familiar with these terms.
- Your points.

LANGUAGE REFERENCE

Language notes

For more detailed notes, see the Business Grammar Guide.

because, as and since

Note the following examples.

e.g. Since we're now all here, I'll begin.

As we're running late, there's no time for more questions.

I missed the presentation because I couldn't find a parking space.

so and therefore

Note the following examples.

e.g. It's time for coffee, so we will have to stop.

Our server isn't working, so could you fax it instead?

It's their responsibility. Therefore, they should pay.

(al)though, even though, in spite of/despite

Note the following examples.

e.g. Although my English isn't very good, I'll try.

Even though I spoke loudly, people couldn't hear at the back.

She is very popular, though I can't understand why.

It didn't go well, in spite of the fact that we prepared carefully.

In spite of being from Hawaii, he prefers to work in the London office.

Useful phrases

First, I'll give you a brief overview of the plans.
Then I'll say a few words about the takeover.
I'd also like to discuss some current market issues.
Our main aim is to increase sales of Fortishka products in Poland.

This table shows projected sales for the coming year.
As you can see from these figures, the projected sales budget is $2 million.
Can everyone see that OK?
Is this better?
Yes, that's much better. Thank you.

With regard to staffing levels, we have 20 full-time staff and ten part-timers.
Moving on to my next point.
That brings me to my next point.
Do you have any questions so far?

As we're running late, I'm afraid I have to stop there.
I'd now like to hand over to Sam.
Sam is going to describe our exciting new product range.
Sam …

How did the talk go?
Not so well unfortunately, in spite of the fact that I prepared carefully.
Even though I used a microphone, some people said they couldn't hear very well.
Well, I thought it went really well.
The feedback was excellent.
I really enjoyed it.

Support materials

UNIT 4 Introducing your company

4 Listening

2 Fill in the form with information about you and your company.

1 Name	**5 Number of employees**
Title _____ **First name** _____ **Surname** _____	1–30 ☐ 101–500 ☐
Position _____	31–100 ☐ 501+ ☐
Business name _____	
Business address _____	**6 Your company's main business activities**
_____ Postcode/Zipcode _____	Agriculture, forestry and fishing ☐
Telephone number _____	Energy and water supply ☐
	Mining, chemicals ☐
2 Type of business	Metal goods, engineering, vehicles ☐
Sole proprietor ☐ PLC ☐	Electronics ☐
Partnership ☐ Subsidiary ☐	Other manufacturing industries ☐
Private Limited	Construction ☐
Company ☐ Other ☐	Retail, distribution, hotels, catering, repairs ☐
	Transport, communications ☐
3 Turnover	Banking, financial, business services ☐
Up to £250,000 ☐ ££5m–£20m ☐	Education, health, government and local authorities ☐
£250,000–£5m ☐ £20m+ ☐	Other ☐
4 Currently involved in import/export	
Export only ☐ Import and export ☐	
Import only ☐ None ☐	

UNIT 6 Competitors

2 Talking point

On page 33, there are five hot tips for beating the competition. Here are five more. How many of them did you guess?

6 **Alert your staff.** The trouble with tip 5 is it can also work against you. Educate your own staff about confidentiality. Train them to ask why callers might need the information they are seeking. Develop a company policy regarding the information that is allowed to be discussed with outsiders.

7 **Allow time.** Don't expect to gather all the information you need to make sound business decisions in a few telephone calls or store visits. Take your time. Avoid the trap of using old information. You should be gathering information on an ongoing basis and routinely adjusting your marketing plan.

8 **Read their brochures.** Competitive literature will tell you many things – including strategy, positioning, products and services, target group and key staff. Check to see if the literature is out of date or up to the minute.

9 **Call them.** Examine how their staff answer the phone and how they approach prospective customers or opportunities. Make a call to them and act like a new business prospect. Have others do the same thing, then compare notes.

10 **It's not all bad.** Not everything the competitor does is right or wrong. Copy the good and avoid the bad.

UNIT 8 Conditions of work

5 Application

Partner B: Use the information below to help **Partner A** complete the chart on page 43.

Job title	Average basic salary	Bonus scheme	Employer's pension contribution	Private health insurance	Company car	Home telephone bill paid	Life assurance cover – x salary
Director			£9,000	Employee and family			
Senior manager	£44,000	£7300			Yes (83%)	Possible	3x
Middle manager			£2,800	Employee only		No	
Senior secretary	£22,500	£2400				No	2x
Skilled operative			£1750	No		No	

UNIT 10 Buying products

2 Practice

Partner B: Use the information below to help **Partner A**, whose details (page 49) are out of date.

> ### Useful language
> We don't stock that size/colour/design any more.
> We used to supply them, but that line is now discontinued.
> We no longer make them in that colour.
> The A444-909 is very similar.

$55
Catalogue no.: A444-908. No longer available. Nearest equivalent **Catalogue no.**: A444-909 Solid brass frame, white dial, bold black. Arabic numerals, quartz movement Diameter: 240mm (9$^1/_2$")

$40
Catalogue no.: A444-911. Line discontinued. Nearest equivalent **Catalogue no.**: A444-912 Quartz movement, black frame, silver dial. Diameter: 240mm (13")

$25
Catalogue no.: A490-89. Unlimited stocks available Battery-operated round quartz wall clock. Red case with easy-to-read graphics and non-scratch glass. Diameter: 240mm (9")

UNIT 15 Service industries

2 Practice

Partner B: You have used Emba Catering recently and know the following about the company.

- They employ more than 2000 staff.
- Staff undertake training in food hygiene and safety, and all food handling. Staff have to pass an annual exam which tests their knowledge of food health and safety regulations.
- Emba Catering have a design department, plan kitchen and restaurant layout, and manage the installation of equipment.

Partner A is about to contact you to find out more about Emba Catering. You would also like to find out from **Partner A** whether he/she as any further information about:

- the scope of Emba's operation
- the number of contracts they have in the region
- their range of services
- their existing customers
- the company's size status.

UNIT 17 Hotels and restaurants

3 Language focus

2 **Partner A** has read an extract (page 78) about who should pay for a business meal. **Partner B's** extract is below.

> As a general rule, the person who invites someone else to a business meal should pay. There are exceptions to this rule, however.
>
> **Example:** You invite another manager to a casual lunch for strictly social reasons. He brings along his wife. In this case, the other manager should offer to pay the bill, since he brought a guest.
>
> **Example:** Two managers agree to have lunch together. Even though one suggested the idea, it is agreed in advance that they will split the bill.

From *The Little Book of Business Etiquette*, by Michael C. Thomsett

UNIT 18 Corporate entertaining

2 Practice

Partner A works for a hospitality company. **Partner B** has a party of 20 to entertain and would like to know the following from **Partner A**.

a What is special about the event.
b How much it costs per person.
c What date the event takes place.
d What time it begins.
e How long it lasts.

Think about what you require.

- A cordoned-off area?
- Use of telephones?
- Toilets?
- Easily accessible free parking?
- Coffee, lunch and tea?
- Bar facilities?

UNIT 20 Meeting procedures

Preparation
Here are some preparation phrases used in meetings.

Getting started
Let's start.
Shall we begin?
I think we should begin.
We only have one hour.

The agenda
Can I take the minutes as read?
Has everyone got an agenda?
These are the four main topics on the agenda.
Let's start with item 1.

Objectives
The main purpose of this meeting is to …
Our aim today is to …
Our main objective is to …

Introducing a topic
As you know …
I think everyone knows that …
The current situation is …
You may not know that …

Bringing people in
Mark, what's your opinion …?
Would you like to begin, Lisa, with …?
I'd believe you wanted to say something about …
I'd like you, John, to outline …

Points of view
I have to say that I'm opposed to …
Are you in favour of …?
I agree with that.

Summarising
John thinks that …
I believe the general view is …
It seems that everyone agrees.

Moving on
Can we move on to the next item?
Let's go on to …
Can we deal with ………… next?

Digressions
Can we deal with that point later?
Can we get back to the main point?
I think we are getting away from the subject.

Concluding
Let's recap.
Is there anything anyone wants to add?
So, we have decided to …

Voting

Shall we vote on the proposal then?
Those in favour? Those against?
Are you abstaining?

Ending the meeting

I suggest we leave it there.
Let's finish there.
I think we can call it a day.
Thank you all for coming.

UNIT 22 Arranging a visit

2 Practice

1 **Partner B's** information: Call **Partner A** for the information you need to finalise his/her itinerary.

Itinerary → → → →

23 Nov	Arrival at Kuala Lumpur airport, on flight number .... , arriving at 2.30pm.
24 Nov	Visit to ....
25 Nov	.... to Ipoh.
26 Nov	Meeting with ....
27 Nov	Return to Kuala Lumpur airport. Singapore Airlines, flight SQ 739 to .... leaving at ....

Useful language

When	will you be arriving in ...?
	does your flight get into ...?
How	are you getting to ...?
Who	do you visit/meet in ...?
What	is [your departure time]?
	is [your ETA]?

UNIT 24 Returning from a business trip

2 Practice

1 **Partner B:** You wrote the notes on page 105. When **Partner A** calls with further questions, reply using the information below.

- See www.mre.gov.br/ingles for background information on Brazil.
- The population of São Paulo is 33 million.
- If São Paulo were an independent country, it would be among the 20 richest worldwide.
- Rio de Janeiro is the same size as Denmark.
- Shipbuilding is a major industry in Rio.
- Minas Gerais has a population of 12 million.
- In Minas Gerais, there are opportunities for export in the textile industry.
- Rio Grande do Sul is one of Brazil's biggest agricultural areas.

UNIT 25 Personal finances

5 Application

1 **Partner B**'s information

SALLY VOIGHT PRODUCTIONS LTD FEES AND EXPENSES

	Current year (£)	Last year (£)
TURNOVER (fee income)	163,141	159,244
EXPENSES		
Secretarial assistant	15,000	–
Wardrobe / clothing	3,666	4,477
Travelling, accommodation & subsistence	8,791	....
Lighting & heating	....	2,281
Motor expenses	2,612	2,163
Telephone & postage		3,446
Professional books, journals & subscriptions	1,350	1,229
	2,566	2,620
Photography	....	....
Company registration expenses	25	40
Company pension plan	36,167	35,429
Director's remuneration	80,604	97,198
Depreciation	300	300
Audit and accountancy	3,100	2,200
Sundry expenses	316	994
	989	880
Cleaning	920	760
Theatre visits & research expenses	....	105

Useful language

How much did she spend on [lighting and heating]?
What's the figure for [theatre visits]?
What's the figure of [£2,566] for?
What does the figure of [£989] represent?

UNIT 27 Payment issues

2 Practice

3 Here is an example of a response that Mr Petersen might write to Ms Ashok.

```
Delete   Reply   Reply All   Forward   Compose   Mailboxes   Get Mail

Dear Ms Ashok                          Your invoice no. 3947

I am writing with reference to your email dated [ ..... ],
relating to the above invoice. According to our records, this
was paid by bank transfer on [ .......... ].

The details are as follows.

Our bank reference: [ ........... ]

Your bank reference: [ ........... ]

Transfer number: [ ........... ]     Date: [ ........... ]

We would be grateful if you could confirm that the payment
has now reached you.

Yours sincerely

Hans Petersen
```

5 Application

2 Useful phrases for **Partner B** when talking to **Partner A** (the customer).

> **Useful phrases**
>
> It was due for payment on …
>
> Payment is now outstanding/overdue.
>
> The delivery note was signed by …
>
> We haven't received anything.
>
> What was the date of your letter/payment?
>
> When can we expect settlement/payment?
>
> Could you sort it out?
>
> We will take no further action providing …
>
> I'll assume everything is OK unless …
>
> I look forward to receiving your payment.

UNIT 29 Presenting facts and figures

5 Application

2 **Partner B:** Your information is more up-to-date than the information **Partner A** has. When **Partner A** calls, help him/her to update his/her records.

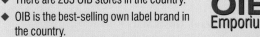

- There are 283 OIB stores in the country.
- OIB is the best-selling own label brand in the country.
- Sales average $487 per square foot.
- The flagship branch in Jojoba hands back more money in refunds than the average OIB branch takes.
- A sale is made every 3.7 seconds.
- It is visited every day by 123,000 people – more than the capacity of a major stadium.
- Three-quarters of a million items are delivered to it every week. A delivery van of food or textiles arrives every 4.25 minutes.
- It sells a ton of fresh and smoked salmon a week.

Audioscripts

UNIT 1 Everyday business contacts

1 Overview

1 a – Is that Paul Smyk?
– Speaking.
– Oh, hello Paul. This is Mary Patel.
– Oh, hi Mary! What can I do for you?
– Is this a good time?
– Yes, it's fine. Go ahead.
– It's just about the report you sent me.
– Oh, my boss Ella Holt is handling that now. And she's on another line at the moment. Can I get her to call you back?
– Er yes, but I have to go out soon. Could you ask her to call me after 4 o'clock?
– Yes, of course. I'll leave her a message.

b – Can I speak to your sales manager, please?
– I'm sorry, he's not in today. It's a public holiday.
– Oh, I see.
– I'm afraid the office is closed. It's Independence Day.
– Er … could you give him a message?
– I won't see him till tomorrow.
– That's OK. Can you tell him that Sam Barekat of United Software called. Ask him to call me when he gets back to the office.
– Yes of course. Could you spell your name, please? And your phone number?

c – Have we covered everything?
– Oh, there is one more thing; someone called Manuel Farkas called for you. He's head of Finance in the Mexico office.
– Ah, what did he want?
– He said he needed some information about the people from CIT.
– Did he leave a number?
– Yes, he's working at home today. He wants you to call back as soon as possible; he has to go out at 12.
– 12 o'clock our time?
– No, Mexican time.
– They're two hours ahead of us. It's about 11.50 local time there now.
– OK, I must go. I may just catch him. Do you have his number?

d – How often do you use English?
– Well, I need it in my job, of course. I can manage OK with colleagues and when we have visitors – in face-to-face situations. But I sometimes have problems on the phone.
– What about emails and reports?
– My written English is OK, but not as good as my spoken English. Luckily I don't often have to write reports.

5 Listening

a – Hello, Milan Roza's phone. Beth May speaking.
– Hello. Is Milan there?
– I'm afraid he's away this week and won't be back until Monday. Have you got his cell number?
– No I haven't. It's Esa Faz here, by the way.
– Hello Esa. OK, it's 405011. I'll let him know you called.
– Thanks, I'll try and call him later today.

b – Hello, Steven Guerola's phone. How can I help you?
– Is he there? It's Lief Andren – I need to speak to him urgently.

– I'm afraid he's in a meeting. He won't be out till 12.30.
– Can you tell him I called, and ask him to get back to me as soon as possible?
– Certainly, Mr Andren.

c – Hello, I'm trying to contact Pat Hersey. It's Max Tuzov.
– Oh, she has another number now, but …
– Could you transfer me?
– I know she's not in yet. I've just tried to transfer another call.
– Then could you ask her to call me on 027782?
– Yes, of course. Sorry, could you give me your name again please?
– It's Tuzov, Max Tuzov – that's T-U-Z-O-V.

d – Hello, Cilla Radley speaking.
– Can I speak to Mr Rymarz, please?
– He's not at his desk. Just a moment, I know he is somewhere in the building …
– Thank you.
– Hello.
– Yes?
– Sorry, I'm afraid he isn't available – he's with some clients. Can I take a message?
– Yes, could you say that Roland Wessels called. I'll call again later.

UNIT 2 Developing contacts

1 Overview

a – Do you have any contacts in Poland?
– Yes, I do. Why?
– My company has been asked to quote for a job there, and we have very little experience of doing business in that part of the world.
– Actually we have quite a few customers in Poland, particularly in the Warsaw area. I know several people who could probably help you. And even if they can't help you themselves, they'll know people who can. Let me send you some names and addresses.
– Thanks, that would be very useful.

b – Hi. It's Ryan Kops here. We met last Friday in Lausanne and you asked me to contact you.
– Oh yes, thanks for calling. You're the guy who's in the office equipment business?
– That's right. How can I help you?
– I wanted to ask you if you know anyone who supplies digital projectors? We need some for our Italian offices.
– How many machines do you need?
– It depends on the deal, of course, but we are planning to install projectors in all of our conference rooms in Rome and Naples.
– I can give you the name of our Italian associate company – there aren't many companies who can compete with them on price or service. I'll give you the sales manager's name.
– Thanks.

c – So what are your accountants like?
– They're very good. Very quick and always professional.
– The reason I'm asking is that our accountants are closing their office next year and we need to find a new firm. It's so difficult to find a replacement.
– Well, I can definitely recommend all of the partners in the firm we use. We had such a big problem last month that I thought it would take at least a week to sort out, but they managed to finish the job in two days.

- Maybe we should talk to them.
- I'll give you their number. I can definitely recommend them.

d
- Hello, is that Rakesh Singh? Yes, it is.
- This is Mary Page. We met a couple of days ago on the flight from Lagos. Do you remember me?
- Ah … Yes, how are you?
- I'm fine, but it's about the problem we were talking about. You said you might be able to help.
- Oh, yes, of course. Go ahead.
- The thing is, we can't get customs clearance for our equipment. It's stuck in a warehouse in Lagos. Apparently there is a problem with the paperwork. Do you know anyone who might be able to help?
- Yes. I've got a few contacts in Lagos.
- Can you give me some names?
- Yes. Hamajo, for example, is a company that could help you. Safiyah Ade is the person you need to talk to. Let me give you her number.
- Thanks.

5 Listening

a
- Hello, it's Tommy Grell of Clearway Printing. Singapore airport, last Tuesday?
- Oh yes! How are you? How did the trip go?
- Very well. We got the business! But we're having some problems with the contracts … and that's why I'm calling you. I remember you said that you have an office there, and you represent several European companies. I wonder whether we could meet for lunch perhaps.
- It would be a pleasure, but I'm afraid I'm very busy for the next couple of months.
- How about the 17th of April – that's the month after next?
- Let me look …Yes, that's fine. Where shall we meet?

b
- Hello, my name is Rick Moffat – we met a couple of days ago at the Detroit Trade Center. You asked me to call you. Do you remember?
- Oh yes, you work for 3X Industries, don't you.
- That's right.
- I'm glad you called. I think we may be able to use that new product you were talking about. I'd like you to talk to our purchasing people. When are you free?
- Unfortunately, I'm just leaving for a trip to Central America for three weeks …
- So you won't be back till next month, and you don't have any time before you go?
- No, I'm afraid my plane is at 6 o'clock this evening. One of my colleagues could call you …
- No, no; it can wait.

c
- Hello, is that Kate Goldsmith?
- Yes, speaking.
- Hi, this is Maria Larsson. We had coffee together the week before last at the computer software exhibition in Dresden. I promised to give you a ring.
- Oh yes, thanks for calling.
- So, when can we meet?
- This week is a bit difficult, and I'm away next week. How about a week on Monday, on the 17th?
- Yes, that's fine. I'll call you nearer the time to arrange the details.
- Good! I'll see you then.

UNIT 3 Out of the office

1 Overview

a
- [Recorded message] You're through to Nistano Supplies. The office is now closed until 8 o'clock tomorrow morning. If you wish to leave a message, please speak after the tone.
- [Person leaving voicemail message] Hello, this is Simon Gusto from Winston Chemicals, with a message for Mr Chan. It's about the parts for the air conditioning unit. I need to speak to him urgently. Could he call me as soon as he gets this message? Thanks.

b
- Hanan Sales. How can I help you?
- Hello, I'm trying to contact Mr Hanan. Is he still in the office?
- No, I'm afraid he has left for the day. He'll be in at 8 o'clock tomorrow morning.
- Do you know how I can get in touch with him? I don't have his mobile number and I have to get hold of him. We're meeting some clients to finalise a deal this evening, and I have the contracts.
- OK. I'll try and get a message to him.
- Thanks, could you ask him to phone me as soon as possible, please?
- Of course; can you give me your name and your phone number?

c
- Hi Pedro, I got your message.
- Thanks for calling back. I've been trying to contact you. Sorry. I was in a meeting and my mobile was off, so my office couldn't contact me.
- I asked for your mobile number, but they wouldn't give it to me. I didn't know how to reach you.
- Sorry about that. They are not allowed to give out our mobile numbers. What's the problem?
- No problem, but we're supposed to be going out to dinner with the people from Mox Engineering this evening.
- Oh, I completely forgot. I'm really sorry. I'll see you at the restaurant in about 40 minutes.

d
- I'm sorry I'm so late. Did you get my message?
- I guessed you were in a meeting or something and couldn't answer your phone.
- Yes, I was in meetings all afternoon, but I did finally manage to check my voicemail. I'm glad you could make it.
- So am I. Now, let me get you something to drink before the others arrive.
- What time will they be here?
- In about ten minutes. We arranged to meet at 8 o'clock.

4 Listening

a Hello. This is a message for Rodney Vale. Could Rodney call Joaquim Delgado at Medina Plastico between 2 o'clock and 5 o'clock tomorrow afternoon. Many thanks.

b Good morning. It's Tony Conway here with a message for Kjell Peterson. Could he please send the brochures which he promised to send me? I haven't received them yet. Thanks.

c Chris. It's Jane Tower here. Can you call me as soon as you get this message. It's about Mary's visit next week. There are a couple of details which we need to sort out.

d I need to talk to your sales manager as soon as possible. Could she call me either on 34909, my office number, or on 45690, which is my mobile number, any time this afternoon. My name is Piero Bellini. That's B-E-L-L-I-N-I.

5 Application
- – Hello, is that Fiona Walker?
- – Yes.
- – This is Ergo Construction Security. We picked up your fax.
- – Oh yes; thank you for calling back. I couldn't get through.
- – Yes, the office is closed. Mr Lopez has just gone home – you missed him by about ten minutes.
- – Have you got his home number?
- – I'm afraid we can't give out private numbers. Shall I get him to call you in the morning?
- – But we're supposed to be going out to dinner with some clients of yours, and I don't have the address of the restaurant. Could you get a message to him?
- – I can try …
- – Would you mind calling him and asking him to call me?
- – Yes of course.

[Later]
- – Hello.
- – Hi Fiona. I got a message to call you.
- – Oh, hi Tony. I've been trying to contact you. Where are we meeting tonight?
- – Oh, sorry, I didn't send you the details. I completely forgot. I'll take a taxi and collect you at 7 o'clock.

UNIT 4 Introducing your company

1 Overview
- a – We're a public limited company. Our annual turnover is just over 180 million euros, and we employ approximately 2,000 people worldwide.
- – Are you part of a group?
- – No, we're an independent company.
- – And what are your main activities?
- – Well, we started 68 years ago making radios. Now, we're a medium-size electronics company, producing a range of electronic sensors. We specialise in sensors for automated systems. But we also make electronic security equipment for the retail market – car alarms, smoke alarms and so on.
- – So, where are your main markets?
- – Our own brand products are sold via retailers in the domestic market. We are also in the export business because the components side sells mainly overseas to foreign manufacturers.
- b – The company is organised in three divisions: production, marketing, and administration. I'm on the finance side, which comes under administration.
- – What does Tommy Hoe do?
- – He's the chief accountant. He's responsible for the sales and purchase ledgers, and for credit control. He has a staff of 12 working for him.
- – Who's Head of Finance?
- – Barbara Stansky; she's the finance director. Tommy Hoe reports to her.
- – And who is in charge of product development?
- – The R&D section is responsible for the early stages, but the real decisions are made by the production manager.
- c – Nowadays most of our production is based in Germany. Our main European plant is in the centre of the country, near Göttingen. We have a five hectare site there, which we own – we have the freehold. We've been there for a little over 12 years. And we have a processing plant about 70 kilometres east of Brussels, near the Dutch border. Both sites are well placed for road and rail links to the main European markets.
- – Where's your head office?
- – It's near Versailles, not far from Paris.

- – Are you a French company?
- – Our parent company is French, yes …
- d – The site is on the coast, outside a village called Hinton. When you get to the village, take the ring road. We're just off the ring road – you'll see the buildings on your right. As you enter the site, you'll see a warehouse in front of you. The car park is the other side of that building. You need to get to the training department, which is in the main building. It's a grey building just beyond the car park. We're on the third floor. When you come out of the lift, go straight ahead, and it's at the end of the corridor. My office is on the left, room 306.

4 Listening
- – Can I ask you a few questions?
- – Yes, of course.
- – OK. Can I have your name?
- – It's Catherine Brass. Brass is spelt B-R-A-S-S.
- – Is that Mrs or Miss?
- – It's Miss.
- – Fine. And what is your job and your company's name and address?
- – I'm a lawyer, and I work for the Masa Partnership. Masa is spelt M-A-S-A. The address is 33 Dock Street, London EC4 B70.
- – Thanks, and can I have your telephone number?
- – Yes, it's 908 897654.
- – Right, you've already answered my next question, so that brings me to turnover. What is your annual turnover, approximately?
- – It's just over 5 million pounds.
- – And you're mainly in the export business?
- – Mainly, yes, but we also buy in services from a French legal firm, so I suppose we're also in the import business.
- – OK. And how many divisions are there in the Masa group?
- – Just one. We're a small business. There are only 13 employees.
- – OK. Thank you. That answers all of my questions.

UNIT 5 Company profiles

1 Overview
- a – What type of company is SEW?
- – It's a so-called public utility company, which means it's owned by the state. The company's main activity is managing water supplies. They run all the water works and sewage plants in this area.
- – And how is the business going?
- – It's going well. Apart from their domestic business, they're now one of the leading exporters of water treatment plants in the country. I heard recently that they're looking to expand that side of their business.
- – Are they making a profit?
- – Yes, they are. The company is a state monopoly, but it's run like a private company, in that they don't receive any government subsidies. Last year they made a profit, before tax, of 333.8 million euros, on a turnover of 1.4 billion.
- b – First of all, let me give you some background information on NPC. We were set up back in 1972 to run the country's electricity supply as a private company. Previously we were a nationalised industry, 100% state-owned.
- – So what are your main activities?
- – Basically we are a power company; we make and distribute electricity.

- Do you own any power stations?
- Yes, we own hydro-electric and wind-powered stations, but the government owns the nuclear plants. We generate approximately 20% of the electricity produced in the country.

c
- When was the company founded?
- I believe it was formed in 1989, when the industry was nationalised and the existing operators were formed into one corporation.
- Is it still state-owned?
- No, not now. It was privatised in 2001. The company was making huge losses and costing the taxpayer a lot of money. The government had to do something.
- So, who owns the company now?
- It's now part of the BAST Group. I believe the parent company owns 52% of the equity. The rest of the share capital is owned by institutional investors and members of the public.

d
- And so what do you do?
- Currently, I'm working as a project manager in a department called CFR, which stands for Coalfield Relocation. It's our job to attract new businesses to coalfields that are closing down because they are no longer profitable. We offer grants, advice and so on.
- Are you funded by the government?
- Yes, we are part of a regional development scheme. We make every effort to attract companies that are looking for low cost industrial sites. So if you are thinking of relocating, call me.

4 Application

- Our main activity is making electricity. We produce it, transport it and deliver it.
- How big is the company?
- Our turnover is about 50 billion euros and we have 10 million customers.
- Is it a state monopoly?
- Yes, it is. But although we are state-owned, we don't receive any subsidies from the government. We are run like a private company.
- How many people do you employ?
- We have 60,000 employees. We generate over 20% of the electricity needed in this country and we export 13% of our total output.
- And so, what do you do? What's your job?
- I am a project manager, which means that it's my job to …

Note The Russian speaker does not pronounce the article in 'I am a project manager'.

UNIT 6 Competitors

1 Overview

a
- I work for a recruitment consultancy. We offer a highly specialised service involving presenting applicants to clients via a web link, in the initial stages. This saves on travel and accommodation expenses and, of course, hours of management time.
- How does this compare with what your competitors offer?
- We believe that we offer a much better service than less specialised companies. In fact, you could say that we don't really have many competitors because our service is unique.
- How do your profits compare with other recruitment companies?
- We're probably more profitable dollar for dollar than other companies because our prices are slightly higher.

But our turnover is far smaller, because we are not as big as they are. In our view, this is an advantage. Size is the least important factor in this market. I don't think you could do what we do on a big scale.

b
- We specialise in mail order. We produce a range of skin care products mainly for women under the SAL brand name.
- Who are your main competitors?
- It's a very tough market. We are competing with companies like Cosmar and Rowdell. Cosmar is one of the largest producers in North America. They rank in the top ten cosmetics companies worldwide. There's a lot of competition, and margins are very tight.
- Are you trying to build up market share?
- Yes, of course. But that's not so easy. The big companies have huge advertising budgets – much bigger than ours.
- So how do you compete?
- We survive because the quality of our products is far higher – we consider ourselves to be the best in the business – and we have scientific test evidence to prove this. We also benefit from strong personal recommendations.

c
- We produce general medical products for the health services, unbranded goods which we supply in bulk.
- What's the competition like in that field?
- In the domestic market our position is quite strong, whereas our competitors are having problems. Their prices are less competitive than ours and they have less developed sales networks. But we're also very active overseas, especially in the Middle East, and that's a much more difficult market for us.
- Are you having to compete with local producers?
- Yes, but the main problem is that we face tough competition from producers in China and South Asia. There is a company called KLT, which has a virtual monopoly in several countries in the Middle East, and we simply can't compete with them.
- Why is that?
- It's mainly a price issue. Their wages costs are far lower than ours, and they run a very efficient operation.

4 Listening

a I work for a toy manufacturing company. It's quite a small company; we only employ 150 people, but we consider ourselves efficient. We have an excellent workforce. Our profitability is far greater than other companies in this business. It needs to be, as the competition is very hard.

b This plant is part of a large mining conglomerate. We are one of the largest producers in the world – we rank in the top ten companies worldwide. At the moment, we have a virtual monopoly in the production of some metals. But, like all our competitors, we are having some economic problems at the moment.

c We produce machinery for the textile industry. Our looms are world-famous. We consider that we offer a far better service for far more reasonable cost than our competitors. However, we are beginning to face tough competition from some new companies in South-East Asia.

d We are a very small family firm of solicitors. We specialise in company conveyancing work. There are only three partners and two salaried assistants. We don't seem to have any problems in getting work. Our services are so specialised.

e AK Build is a very large construction company. We are currently very active in Central America, where we have a number of major projects ongoing. Unfortunately, we've recently lost a couple of big orders. Our currency is so strong that we can't compete on price.

UNIT 7 Your personal background

1 Overview

a – What are you doing these days?
  – I've got a job with a TV company. It's part time but I'm hoping to get a full-time job with them when there's a vacancy. I was made redundant last year, so I was lucky to get another job so quickly. Did you know that we've moved?
  – No. Where are you living now?
  – We have an apartment in the centre of town. Anna likes it because it's near our daughter.
  – How is Anna?
  – She's fine. You must come and have dinner with us soon.

b – Geoff, how have you been?
  – Very well. But I don't like the summer so much – I always suffer from hay fever.
  – Yes, it's been a bad year for hay fever.
  – Anyway, what are you up to these days? Do you still work for DBS?
  – Yes. In fact, I'm working with Omar Marat. Do you remember him?
  – Yes, of course. Hasn't he retired yet?
  – No. I don't think he'll ever retire!

c – So, where were you born?
  – In the south of Spain, near Marbella. My wife and children still live there. I now live in Valencia.
  – Why did you move to Valencia?
  – I have friends and business contacts there, so I could find freelance work more easily.
  – Do you see your wife and children often?
  – Most weekends. But they are moving to Valencia next month.
  – Oh, that's good. I didn't know you were self-employed.
  – Yes, I have been for a couple of years now. .

d – How's your husband?
  – He hasn't been well. He's had a bad back and has been in quite a lot of pain. He also suffers from arthritis.
  – I'm sorry to hear that.
  – Yes, we even had to cancel our holiday this summer because of it. We were planning to go on a cruise. Have you ever had to cancel a holiday at the last minute? I don't recommend it, even if you *are* covered by insurance!
  – Sounds like you have had a difficult time.
  – Yes. Let's hope next year will be better.

4 Application

– Tom … good to see you! What are you doing these days? Are you still in the food business?
– No, not any more. They closed the factory down last year, and everyone was given the choice either to move to London or take redundancy. I'm not far off retirement age – I'm 58 now – and I didn't want to move to London, so I took the redundancy package.
– How long ago was that?
– About six months.
– And how have you been? Are you enjoying it?
– Oh, it's not too bad. I enjoy reading and I still collect antiques. So I keep busy and I'm in good health.
– I'm sure … Do you still go on walking holidays?
– Oh, yes – I'm not too old for that yet! By the way, did I tell you that we've moved?
– No, you didn't. Where to?
– We, er, we sold our house and we've just bought a small bungalow. I'm really pleased with it. The house was too big

for us now the children are grown up. Caroline likes it too, because it's got a big garden.
– How is Caroline?
– She's OK. As you know, she's very keen on riding … so she spends a lot of her time at the stables. The only problem is that she gets quite a lot of back pain, which slows her down a bit. Anyway, what's your news?

UNIT 8 Conditions of work

1 Overview

a – What kind of salary package have they offered you?
  – Well, there's a bonus scheme, which is on top of the basic salary.
  – Is it good?
  – I think so. In my case it's worth about a month's salary?
  – And do you get a company car?
  – No, but the company pays 26% towards the cost of buying a car.
  – Do they contribute to the running costs?
  – Only if you're on company business, then you can claim expenses.
  – Well, that seems fair. And do they pay your phone bill?
  – No they don't. Only the sales people get company phones, and of course their bills are paid by the company.
  – What about a clothing allowance?
  – No, office staff don't get anything. Some manual grades get an allowance for overalls.

b – We were just clearing up when the fire started. We'd just finished work.
  – And I had just left the office. I was actually going down in the elevator when the alarm went off.
  – You are lucky you weren't trapped in the elevator.
  – I know. When I got outside, smoke was coming out of the windows on the top floor. I tried to call you, but there was no answer. I thought you'd gone home.
  – I was still trying to get out of the building when you phoned!

c – Can I ask you a few questions about your office? I'm doing a survey of working conditions.
  – Sure. Go ahead.
  – First, do you think that there is enough space for everyone?
  – Yes, there's no problem with space – there's plenty of room for everyone, and the office is well ventilated.
  – What about the lighting? Is it bright enough for you to read comfortably?
  – Yes it's fine, all the lights are adjustable.
  – Is there anything you don't like?
  – Yes, there are a few things. Some of the work surfaces are too small to work on comfortably. And some of the shelves are too high for me to reach.
  – OK …
  – And in my opinion there's too little leg room under the desks.
  – Right. Anything else?
  – Er, yes … There are too few power points. And it can be quite noisy; we're on a main road and it can be noisy when we open the windows.

3 Language focus

3 SOFIA: I'd already gone home. I left the building at about 5 o'clock, I think. There were still quite a few lights on in people's offices then.

MONA: I was still in the building. I was having a cup of coffee in my office when I thought I could smell burning. When I heard the alarm, I ran down the fire escape.

ANDREW: I was just putting my coat on. I was about to leave the building when I heard the alarm. I came outside and saw smoke coming out of a top floor window.

KHALID: I was coming down in the lift when the alarm went off. I'd just finished for the day. I got out of the lift on the second floor, because I thought it would be safer to walk down the stairs. When I got outside, a huge crowd of people had gathered. They were pointing at the smoke pouring out of a window on the top floor.

4 Listening

Speaker 1
Well, my employer provides medical care, free of charge, for myself and my family. There are limits to it, but it works out pretty well. And there's also a pension plan where, if I stay in my organisation for 20 years, I can retire at half pay.

Speaker 2
The bank – we have a subsidised restaurant for all the staff. And every year in December we get a bonus – that is, two months' salary in addition to the December salary. It is paid on the 10th of every December.

Speaker 3
My company offers me a lot of very good perks. I have a clothing allowance, a company car , a regional weighting allowance. I have private medical care. I also get life insurance.

Notes
i   The speakers are in order: American, Sri Lankan, English.

UNIT 9 Job descriptions

1 Overview

a – Have you met the new finance director?
  – Yes, I knew her when she was with Abets. She was the consumer research manager there – in charge of the retail side.
  – Hmm, what's she like?
  – I like her. She's very bright, hard-working. She's a good leader.
  – She's certainly very well qualified. She told me once that she had studied law at university and then moved on to accountancy. One of the best things about her is that she is very approachable and willing to listen.

b – As marketing manager, I'm responsible for the day-to-day running of the department.
  – What does that involve?
  – Well, I have to liaise with the product managers, with production, and the sales people of course. It's my job to coordinate our marketing activities. So, I spend a lot of my time in meetings, listening to people, advising people.
  – What sort of back-up do you have?
  – I have a staff of seven, including my assistant manager. And I share a PA.
  – Do you have much to do with the finance side?
  – Yes. Budgeting and preparing revenue forecasts are part of the job.

c – Do you recommend Magdalena?
  – Yes, I do. She has the qualifications we're looking for and I think she'd fit into the organisation well.
  – What's her background?
  – She trained in IT and has three years' experience as a business analyst, working in a bank on the telecommunications side.

– Actually, I think I met her at a conference once. Is she tall and slim with dark hair?
– Yes, that's her.

4 Listening

SONYA REED (SR): I'm secretary to the production director. The job involves, first, keeping his diary, which is most important, so that when people ring and ask 'Can I see him?' I say 'Yes' or 'No' or whatever; contacting other people for meetings, which in this place means meetings to discuss meetings; keeping his files straight; arranging lunch appointments and travel, which he does a fair bit of in his job. As far as the factory floor is concerned, the only people I really have dealings with are the chief engineer. Apart from that, I don't have a lot to do with the factory floor, really. The office and the factory are kept rather separate, unfortunately.

INTERVIEWER (I): How long have you been here?

SR: Ten years.

INT: And always the same job?

SR: No, I haven't always been in the same job. I started off in the maintenance department as the clerk. It was my job to order all the spares for the machines and, again, organise all the daily routines, checking that everything was correct when the orders came in. From there, the chief engineer was made works manager, so I went with him, and then he became production director, so I went with him again. So I haven't always been in the same job, no, but always secretary to the same person.

INT: Do you come from Oxford?

SR: No, Banbury.

INT: So that's not far away?

SR: No, 20 miles or so.

INT: So, what do you do in your free time, when you're not working?

SR: Not a lot, really. Housework, cooking. I've got two children, and a dog and a cat … so really, I haven't got a lot of spare time. If we have any spare time, we usually go out for meals, or we just meet up with friends. But I haven't really got a hobby. It takes up most of my time being here, at work, and doing housework at home.

UNIT 10 Buying products

1 Overview

a – Hello. I'd like to order 200 clocks, please – the ones with a wooden case on the first page of your brochure. The catalogue reference number is 12/47-A9.
  – Oh, I'm sorry, that model is out of stock. We will have some new stock in two days.
  – Do you have anything else that is similar?
  – Yes … we also supply the 'Caspian' clock. It is a more traditional-looking clock; it also comes in a wooden case.
  – How much is it?
  – It's slightly cheaper. Let me check. Yes, it's 67 euros. You can check all our prices on our website, by the way. You can also order direct from the site.

b – Can I check the availability of your plastic storage crates? Do you stock the full product range featured on your website? And do you have them in all sizes?
  – Yes, we can supply most items from stock.
  – OK, I'd like to order 40 medium-sized crates – half in green and half in blue.
  – I'm afraid we no longer make them in those colours.
  – But on your website it says they're available in blue and green.

- I'm sorry about that. We need to update the site. Crates from the current range only come in orange or red.
- Hmmm … How soon could you deliver them?
- Delivery usually takes three working days in Europe.

c
- Can you help me? You used to stock a watch with a white face and black Arabic numerals.
- That's right, the 'Classic'.
- Yes, that's it. Do you still stock it?
- No, I'm afraid that line is discontinued.
- That's a shame. It was extremely good value.
- Yes, it used to be very popular. The nearest equivalent is the 'Rex' – it is very similar.

d
- We manufacture a range of trampolines. Our products are highly competitive and we offer a money-back guarantee. We also offer free delivery and a highly efficient aftersales service.
- Do you make trampolines specifically for children?
- We used to, but we had one or two safety problems with them, so we don't any more. For children we recommend the 'Funster' trampoline. It's big enough for all the family to use, but it's round – which makes it safer.
- How big is it?
- The frame is 3.5 metres square – it covers an area of 12 square metres. And the bed of the trampoline is 3 metres in diameter.

4 Listening

a We make industrial clothing – heavy-duty overalls, footwear and so on. All our products are durable – they have to be able to stand the usage they get. Our clothing is also highly competitive in terms of price. We're market leaders in Europe, so we can afford to work with narrow margins. You won't get better value anywhere else.

b We're a small company. We produce and sell educational toys for children – musical instruments, junior calculators, clocks that can be taken apart, that sort of thing.
Our products have to be well-designed and constructed. Teachers don't want equipment that falls apart as soon as it's used. But every item carries a three-month guarantee anyway.

c We are the second largest manufacturer of furniture in the country. We produce furniture and fittings for offices, schools, homes and kitchens. Almost one-third of our turnover comes from abroad. Our products have a reputation based on excellent quality, extremely reasonable prices and highly original designs.

d We supply conservatories and greenhouses in kit form. An average structure is about 90% glass, with an aluminium frame. The base is made of concrete and we lay that as part of the service. Our best-selling model, the Sun Lounge Conservatory, covers an area of 16.5 square metres. But all our lines are very popular. They're stylish and they're also a very economical way of adding an extra room to your house. All of our conservatories are very reasonably priced.

UNIT 11 Product descriptions

1 Overview

a
- How long have you been making hang-gliders?
- About 15 years. We started off making all-purpose models, but now we specialise in the high performance end of the business. And now we're the largest manufacturer of gliders for high altitude and competitive flying. We've built up a lot of expertise in this area.

- Are your gliders normally made to order?
- No, we mainly produce 'standard' models which come in a range of colours and trims; there are a lot to choose from.
- Do you have a low-budget range?
- Yes. For two years now we've been producing an 'off-the-shelf' line available at the lowest possible prices. It's been very popular.

b
- Excuse me, could you tell me if this canoe is suitable for a beginner, a child?
- Yes, it is. It's particularly good for beginners because it is very stable. These canoes range in size from 3 metres 80 to 4 and $^3/_4$ metres – that's about 15 and a $^1/_2$ feet. The junior models are over there. How old is your child?
- She's 12. She hasn't been going canoeing for very long.
  Well, these canoes are ideal. We've been selling them for 20 years. They're safe and they're light, which makes them easy for children to carry.
- How much are they?
- They range in price from 400 to 500 dollars, depending on size and finish.

c
- On average we produce about 2000 tents a week. The process is mainly mechanised, but there are stages that are done by hand. All our fabrics are supplied pre-dyed.
- So how are they made?
- The first step is for us to treat the fabrics with a water-resistant solution and a fire retardant. Then, when the fabric is dry, it's cut into panels. These are then sewn together, and after that, the joins are reinforced with tape and at this stage the groundsheet is attached. Most of our lines have built-in groundsheets, which are glued to the upper section. The next step is to put in the eye-holes and zips. And then, finally, the tent is connected to the frame.
- What's the frame made of?
- We use aluminium poles or fibre-optic rods.

3 Language focus

3 First, the nylon is cut into panels, which are sewn into long strips of fabric, called gores. The edge of each panel is folded back on itself, laid on the next folded edge, and then all four layers of fabric are sewn through twice by machine. The joins are reinforced by heavy-duty nylon tapes, and it's these tapes, rather than the nylon panels, that carry the loads suspended beneath the air bag, or 'envelope' as we call it. At this stage of construction, the envelope has large holes at the top and bottom. The top hole allows the pilot to release air rapidly when he or she wants to descend or land. It's controlled by a movable fabric construction that resembles a parachute – and that's, in fact, what it's called. Stainless steel wires are used to connect the envelope to a frame, which supports the burner. Stronger steel wires run down from the burner frame to support the basket, which is usually made from cane and willow. Other materials, including plastics and aluminium, have been tried as substitutes, but they aren't as good as the traditional material – they aren't flexible enough, and they aren't as durable.

UNIT 12 Faults and breakdowns

1 Overview

a
- Service department. Helen Mladic speaking. How can I help you?

- Hello. Tomas Brett here. It's about the batch of smoke alarms you delivered last week. The reference is B7/402-SM.
- Let me get the order up on screen … Right, here it is. How can I help you?
- I'm afraid they all seem to be faulty. We've had three false alarms in the last 24 hours.
- I'm very sorry about this. Do you have any idea what is causing the problem?
- No, I don't. But as a result we don't have proper fire protection and our building insurance is probably invalid.
- I really apologise for this. I'll make sure the faulty alarms are replaced immediately.
- Thanks. I'd really appreciate it if you could send the replacements today. The courier could then take away the faulty units.

b
- I'm just calling to let you know that we have been very happy with the new high-speed scanning machine you installed last month. It's excellent.
- That's good to hear. We've had very good feedback from a number of our clients.
- I'm not surprised. It's an outstanding machine. We'll certainly be in contact if we need to buy any more.
- Thank you for that. I appreciate it.

c
- We've received some complaints from the firm that is renting the warehouse complex. They say that they have a long list of things that need sorting out.
- Really?
- Yes … Apparently some of the windows don't shut properly, and the air-conditioning in the offices doesn't work, the paintwork in the showroom is badly scratched, and there's some damage to the roof – some parts need to be mended urgently. Oh, and since they moved in, the lift has broken down three times.
- What!
- They are very unhappy about the situation. They want to know what we're going to do about it.
- But we employ an estate agent to handle this!
- I contacted the guy who sent this report, and he said that he had already called the agents several times, but they haven't done anything.
- I'll call the agents immediately.

d
- I tried to contact the person who made the complaint, but he was out … so I talked to some other people where he works. They say that everything is working fine now. Overall, they are very pleased with the job we have done for them.
- That's good news. I was rather surprised that they weren't happy, because we've had excellent feedback from our other customers.

3 Language focus

3
- I've just received the result of the check on the car, and there are a couple of things that need to be sorted out before I agree to buy it.
- What are they?
- First of all, there's some damage to the paintwork, particularly on the bonnet – there are some long, deep scratches. Then the bumper is loose – it's almost hanging off, apparently. They also noticed that the petrol tank is leaking. It's a small leak, but it obviously needs sorting out.
- Yes, of course. Is there anything else?
- Yes, the petrol gauge is stuck on zero. The windows don't close properly – they're very stiff, and they keep sticking. One of the headlights doesn't work; they think it's to do with faulty wiring.

- Did they say anything about the gearbox?
- No problem there. But there were one or two other small things – you'll see them when I send you the report.

UNIT 13 The services you provide and use

1 Overview

a
- We handle the factory cleaning ourselves, and all the maintenance of the machinery and production equipment is done by our own people.
- What about office equipment?
- Some we buy and some we lease. All of our computer equipment is leased, and we have a full service contract with our providers.
- What does the contract include?
- It covers all routine and emergency call-outs, but not spare parts.
- But it covers labour?
- Yes.
- Do you think it's good value?
- Yes I do. The call-out time is about an hour, and the engineer will even come out on a Sunday if necessary. The other big advantage is that if they need to take a machine away to fix it, they provide a replacement.

b
- Do you handle your own security?
- No. We've outsourced all responsibility for security to a company called Cruz Secure.
- What about your logistics?
- The same thing. It's handled by an outside contractor. We find that it's more efficient to subcontract these services so we can concentrate on our core business. We're not good at organising transport and deliveries; it's not our area of expertise.

c
- We must get this photocopier replaced. It's always breaking down.
- Are you going to buy one?
- We're not sure. What do you think?
- Well, I reckon it's more convenient to lease copiers – but sometimes it's a little more expensive.
- What's the cost of leasing one of these, do you know?
- Based on what we pay for a similar model – we have five machines – the rental would be about 20 euros per week, per machine.
- Hmm, how does that compare with buying one?
- It's difficult to make a direct comparison because we have a service agreement included in the lease. I suppose if you shop around you could buy one for about 3,000 euros.

d
- As you know, we urgently need to have our water-cooling systems updated.
- Well, the list price of the equipment you need is in the region of 19,900 dollars. But at the moment we're offering a discount of 10% on orders over 15,000 dollars. So the final price would be about 18,000 dollars, just under.
- What about the installation? Could we do it ourselves?
- You could, if you have the expertise. But I would recommend that we do it for you.

3 Listening

a The service is heavily subsidised by the company. More than 60% of the workforce here are women and a lot of them couldn't work if there wasn't a crèche. I certainly couldn't do my job – at least, not without more money. For me it's essential, but the prices they charge mean that it's very good value too.

b People use us because they've heard of us. We have a good reputation – we don't overcharge, and that's rare in the breakdown business. The downside is that we get more calls than we can handle – so the waiting time is often longer when you call us. We don't subcontract work; we always answer our own calls.

c For us, it's a very cost-effective solution. The total amount that we spend on maintaining our sites may be a dollar or two more than when we used to do it ourselves, but we save a lot of time and energy – we can concentrate on making TV programmes, which is what we're good at and how we make money. There are fewer distractions.

d They're expensive, of course, but I think it's worth it. They offer an excellent service, one that's really useful. If you need to have a parcel delivered on the other side of the world by lunchtime tomorrow, they're the people to call. You know it'll be there.

UNIT 14 Service issues

1 Overview

a – You said the money would be transferred by the end of the week. I've just checked our account and it still hasn't arrived.
  – That's strange. It should have arrived in your account by now. It was sent on Monday.
  – Well, as far as I know, we haven't received it yet.
  – I'm very sorry about this. Can you give me the details again and I'll look into it.
  – Thanks. It's for invoice TS 11472, dated May 22nd.
  – OK, I'll find out what has happened and I'll call you straight back.

b – But you promised us next-day delivery two days ago.
  – Yes, I'm very sorry about this. I've checked with the driver. He says that he delivered it on Tuesday, the date it was due. Apparently, Mr Hazari signed for it.
  – Are you sure? According to our stores manager, we haven't received anything from you this week. We don't have a Mr Hazari working here.
  – Oh, I'm very sorry about this. It seems as if we have delivered the package to the wrong address. I'll find out what has happened and I'll call you back.

c – I'm very sorry that we've had to cancel the course due to insufficient demand.
  – But it's supposed to start next week.
  – Yes, but I'm afraid only 12 people have enrolled.
  – I'm not happy about this. You really could have let us know earlier. Are you planning to run another course?
  – Well, we have another course planned for next month which will definitely go ahead. I can put you down for that course and offer you a 25% discount. I can only apologise for this.
  – Hmm. That sounds reasonable. Let's do that.

d – Hi, Gina. I'd like to apologise for not delivering your order this week.
  – What was the problem?
  – We're almost out of raw materials, on account of the docks strike in Derbent.
  – I'm sorry to hear that, but you could have contacted us earlier. You must have known that your stocks were running low, and I had heard about the possibility of a strike a couple of weeks ago.
  – Yes, I do apologise.
  – We've had to stop one of our machines as a result of this. So what's the current situation?
  – Well, the good news is that the strike has now ended – things are getting back to normal.

4 Listening

  – Fast Parcel. Ernst Capel speaking. Can I help you?
  – I hope so. My name's Tara Vene, from the Tempest Shipping Agency. We sent a parcel on your 48-hour service to Lublin in Poland last week, and I've just heard that it hasn't arrived yet. We are very worried about it.
  – I see. Have you got the parcel reference number there?
  – Yes, it's 672/987-POL.
  – OK. I'll check what's happened to the parcel and I'll call you back within 15 minutes. It certainly should have arrived by now.
  – Thank you.
[Later]
  – Tara Vene.
  – Hi. It's Ernst Capel here. I've checked with the driver and he says that he delivered the parcel. He did say, however, that he forgot to ask for a signature, so I'm sorry, but I don't know who actually took delivery of the parcel.
  – Oh, as far as I know, our customer hasn't received it. I just hope that no one's stolen it – it was a very valuable consignment. The driver should have been more careful. I'm surprised that he was prepared to hand over the parcel without getting a signature.
  – As I said, I'm very sorry.
  – OK, but I'm afraid we'll have to make a claim under the terms of your guarantee. Can you send me the forms?
  – Yes, I understand. I'll send them immediately, but let me try and find out what has happened to your consignment.

UNIT 15 Service industries

1 Overview

a – How big is the company?
  – I'd describe it as medium-sized. Did you know that it's part of the Nalp group? The company employs about 150 people and is very strong in the south of the country.
  – What kind of customers do they have?
  – A wide range – from very small to very large. They have a couple of major customers such as ABL and Lloyds.
  – Do you have any idea what their ABL contract is worth?
  – According to their sales manager, it's worth 400,000 dollars.
  – That's impressive!

b – It's a new company that specialises in recycling glass containers like bottles and jars.
  – How does the service work?
  – The company collects empty containers in special bins, cleans them, and returns them ready for re-use. Containers that are broken or cracked are recycled.
  – How much do they charge for the service?
  – User companies pay a fixed price for a guaranteed supply of bottles. In our case, we hope to save more than 30% of the cost of new bottles by using the service.
  – That's a big saving!

c – Can I check that your commission is still 1.5%?
  – Um, actually, our charges went up last April. They are now 1.75% of debts recovered. Would you like me to send you a copy of our charges?
  – Yes, please. I understand that you also provide a credit control service.
  – Yes, we do.
  – Could you also let us know your fees for that?

d – What services does Emba Catering provide?
  – They run in-house canteens, cater for conventions, and organise sandwich and snack services.
  – That must require a lot of staff.

- It does. Apparently they employ 2,000 people, but many are part-time and casual workers.
- Do they have a good record on hygiene?
- According to the person I spoke to, all staff members are tested regularly, but only 10% pass.
- Who did you speak to?
- Their public relations manager.
- Surely that can't be right.
- Maybe they said only 10% fail.
- That sounds more likely, but it still seems a lot.
- I agree.

4 Listening

a You should have called us earlier. We had one of our lorries in your area this morning and we could have picked up the lot. You can either bring the goods over to the depot, or wait until next week's collection. Either way, there's no extra charge.

b I'd be grateful if you could send the share certificate to me as soon as possible. Can I check, by the way, that your commission is still 1.5%?

c Could you do a search on some property that we're interested in? I'll send you the relevant papers this afternoon. And could you let us know your fees for this kind of work?

d We'd like you to advise us on security management. We need to set up a system of strict access control to data. We are very worried that unauthorised users can get into our system at the moment. I have heard you are an expert in password management.

e We'd like you to give us a quote for a policy that would cover all business travel by company personnel. It should cover all risks and be as flexible as possible.

UNIT 16 Looking after visitors

1 Overview

a – Where do you usually take foreign visitors for lunch?
- It depends. I normally take them to a fish restaurant near the river – it's only five minutes from the office. The food is very good and the staff are friendly.
- Do you ever take them sightseeing?
- Yes occasionally, when there's time.
- And what if they want to go out in the evening?
- Sometimes we take them into town for a night out, but more often we just recommend some places.
- Don't you go with them?
- No, not very often. After a day of meetings I'm usually exhausted.
- They probably need a break, too!

b – Remember to shake hands when you're introduced. And it's a good idea to carry your business cards – people will expect one.
- OK, and what should I wear?
- It's an informal occasion, so wear something smart but casual.
- I don't need to wear a suit?
- Oh no, that's not necessary.
- And should I take a gift?
- You don't have to, but it would be a good idea. Something typical from your country would be best.
- I'm afraid I didn't bring anything with me. I'll get some chocolates from the gift shop.
- That will be fine. We'd better watch the time. We mustn't be late.
  OK. Thanks for your help.

c – I was thinking of getting tickets to the opera. Or would you rather do something else?
- I'd love to go to the opera. But, really, I'm easy. What would you prefer to do?
- Well, there's an excellent production of *Rigoletto* on at the moment. We could go on Tuesday next week.
- Um … Tuesday is a bit difficult. I was hoping to visit my cousin then.
- Are you free on any other days next week?
- Yes, I'm free every evening, except Tuesday.

d – Were you planning on doing anything special tonight?
- Not really. Why?
- I thought we could have dinner.
- That would be great.
- So, when do you finish work?
- At six.
- OK, I could book a table for 8 o'clock and meet you at your hotel at, say, 7.30?
- That would be good; it gives me time to have a shower and get changed.
- Is there anything you don't eat, by the way? I was thinking of going to a Korean restaurant.
- No, I'm always happy to try something new. I've never had Korean food.
- Fine. I'll book a table and see you at 7.30.
- See you then.

4 Listening

- Where do you usually take your clients when they are in Monaco?
- We usually take them to one of the restaurants near the office for lunch. We have some very good French, Italian and Tex-Mex restaurants nearby. If it's for dinner we usually go into the centre. There's a great fish restaurant in Princess Caroline Street, which is one of my favourite places. Unfortunately, we don't go there as much as I would like.
- Do you often have people staying over the weekend?
- Not so often. We do occasionally. I live in the centre of town, so I'm very happy to show them the sights. A lot of our visitors are very keen to see the Palace. Then there's football – I support Monaco.
- Is that a good idea?
- Yes, why not? The atmosphere is great, even if you don't like football. The problem is, customer visits rarely take place when Monaco are playing.

UNIT 17 Hotels and restaurants

1 Overview

a – Shall we have a drink before we eat? What about the lobby bar?
- Good idea, but let's find somewhere to leave our coats first.
- So, did you manage to speak to John?

- Yes, I talked to him this morning. I told him about the conference, and said we were having problems finding a hotel.
- What did he say?
- He recommended the Avio. He says it has excellent conference facilities. He told me to get back to him for some other ideas, if the Avio is booked up.

b A: Right, what can I get you Frances?
  B: I'd like a soft drink, please. An orange juice.
  A: Aha, Mike?
  C: I'll have a glass of white wine, please.

A: Kevin?

D: A beer please. But let me get them. You bought the drinks earlier. What would you like?

A: That's very kind of you. I'd like a beer too please, just a small one. [Speaks to barman] Did you get all that?

E: Yes I did. Take a seat and I'll bring the drinks over to you.

D: Thanks, and could you put the drinks on the bill. I'll settle up later.

E: Yes, of course.

c A: Are you ready to order?

B: Yes, I think we are. J. J. – you said you would have the chicken.

C: That's right, I'll have the special chicken dish, with some vegetables please – spinach and green beans.

D: A rump steak for me, please, and can I have it with a green side salad.

B: And I'd like the prawn salad as a main course, please.

A: Certainly. And how would you like your steak?

D: Oh, … medium rare, please.

A: Thank you. And would you like a starter?

B: No, thank you. We're in a bit of a hurry.

A: OK. I'll tell the chef. Can I get you anything else?

B: Just a large bottle of sparkling mineral water please.

4 Application

RALPH: Mary, Hiroshi. Please sit down. I'll just get the menu. OK. This looks fine, although I don't know if we've got time for three courses.

MARY: I'm not so hungry. Maybe I'll just have a starter. The fresh fruit platter sounds good.

HIROSHI: I think I'll have the salmon, and the chicken peri peri to follow. What about you Ralph?

RALPH : The onion soup, and then a steak. Excuse me, we are ready to order.

WAITER: Certainly sir, what would you like?

RALPH : One fresh fruit platter.

MARY : Actually, can I change my mind and have the prawn salad instead? And can I have it as a main course?

WAITER : Yes, of course.

RALPH : We'd both like starters. The salmon, and an onion soup for me, and a chicken peri peri and a sirloin steak to follow.

WAITER : How would you like your steak?

RALPH : Medium rare, please. Could you be as quick as possible, please. I'm afraid we don't have very much time. And can we order some drinks?

WAITER : Yes, of course. What would you like?

UNIT 18 Corporate entertaining

1 Overview

a – I have a party of 20 to entertain on the 17th. Do you have anything for that date?
 – Yes, the Metro pro–celebrity tennis tournament is on that weekend. and I think we still have some hospitality suites available.
 – And do you recommend it?
 – Yes, it's usually very good, lots of big names – Kojo Arawi is playing this year.
 – Ah … where's it held?
 – At the Metropolis tennis club.
 – Hmmm … it could be what we're looking for. What time does it start?
 – Play begins at 10.30, but corporate guests have access to their suites from 9 onwards.
 – And how much is it?

 – It depends on what you want. The basic package we provide includes the suite, TV monitors and a sit-down lunch. It also covers admission charges, parking and so on.
b – The event begins at 10am and lasts four hours. It's always a great show. This year there will be at least 100 aircraft.
 – And where are you located?
 – In the main hospitality complex. We're conveniently located close to all the main attractions. We can offer a superb view of the proceedings.
c – I'm calling about the hospitality package you offer for the clothes show. Can I make a booking?
 – Do you have all the details?
 – Yes, I'd like the standard package, but with one small change?
 – Yes, of course.
 – We're not sure about the four-course lunch. We think it might put everyone to sleep.
 – Why not have a cold buffet instead?
 – That's what we were thinking.
 – OK, I'll arrange that …
d – That was a good shot!
 – And a great save! What's the score, by the way?
 – Two–nil, I think.
 – Do you ever play yourself?
 – No, I prefer watching. Do you play?
 – Yes, when I can. When's half time?

4 Application

 – We are centrally located – there's an excellent view of the 18th hole from our marquee.
 – Right, that sounds excellent. So can I make a booking for nine people on June the 23rd?
 – Yes, of course. You've got our brochure?
 – Yes, I have. I'd more or less like to have the standard package, but can I make a couple of changes?
 – Yes, of course. No problem. What would you like?
 – OK, we'd basically like the full service although I'm not so worried about the flowers. Special viewing area, parking facilities, etc. … Yes, of course. Programmes, yes. And we'd like to have coffee in the morning, but isn't a full lunch rather heavy?
 – If you like, we could do a cold buffet instead.
 – Hm … that's a good idea. Oh yes, and with regards to the bar, please put all the drinks on our bill.
 – Right. Have you thought of having music, by the way? We can provide an excellent pianist.
 – I'm not sure that's such a good idea when there are only going to be nine of us. And it might disturb the golfers! Can we leave that?
 – Sure.
 – I'll confirm this next week. Thanks for all your help.

UNIT 19 Setting up meetings

1 Overview

a – Hi Donna. We need to set up a meeting to discuss the sales report. Would you be able to meet on Wednesday?
 – Let me just check my diary. Ummm … it looks as if Wednesday is going to be difficult. And I have some interviews on Thursday.
 – What about Friday?
 – It depends on what time. I'm busy in the morning.
 – Well, it looks as though the conference room isn't available till after lunch anyway, so shall we meet at 2.30?

– Yes, that suits me. I'll reserve the room. Can you let everyone know?

– Sure. I'll email everyone when I get back to the office.

– Let me know if there any problems. I can make it later in the afternoon if necessary.

b   Jason, this is Leila. I'm calling to let you know that there's going to be a meeting to talk about the new contract; Norman would like you to attend, if you can. It's on Friday the 23rd, and … er … we're meeting at 10am. This office isn't big enough for all of us, so we're having it at Marta House, in room 406. Hope you can make it. Could you get back to me by the weekend at the latest? Actually, no don't worry about that – if I don't hear from you, I'll assume that everything is OK.

c   – Hi Dieter, I thought I'd better call you about the management meeting.

– Is there a problem?

– Next week's management meeting has been put off till Thursday. Apparently the auditors are using the conference room.

– Will it still be at the usual time?

– No, it's been put back till 3.15 and moved to the boardroom. Can you still make it?

– Er … I have an appointment then, but I'm sure I can move it.

– Shall I send you confirmation of the new details?

– No, don't worry about that – but I do need an agenda.

– Didn't you receive one?

– No, I don't think so.

– Oh, I'm sorry; I'll send you a copy today.

d   – Are you still OK for the 27th? Did you get my email?

– Yes I did. I was going to ring you later today. We're having some problems at this end. Bruna is still in Estonia working on the Freshet project.

– Is she going to be able to make the meeting?

– I don't think so. She doesn't think she'll be back in time.

– That's a shame. I suppose we'd better postpone it. Will she be back by the weekend?

– I hope so.

– OK. I suggest that we all meet up for lunch on Friday, at my office, if you don't mind.

– That suits me.

3 Listening

– Hello.

– Ramond, hi. It's Phillip here. Thanks for your message. I thought I'd better call you as things are getting even more complicated. I'm terribly sorry, but I'm having some more problems at my end. I've just heard that the Mexican guys are very keen to have a look at our Belgian plant as well, and they were told that I would be available to take them at the weekend. No one consulted me! Anyway, they're very important potential clients, so I'll have to go.

– Don't worry, I understand. These things happen. So, are we going to be able to get together? How long are you going to be away for?

– Just till Sunday morning. They're leaving early on a direct flight from Brussels to Madrid. I'll see them off and catch a later flight to London.

– Is that to Heathrow?

– Yes.

– OK, then, we'd better meet at the airport on Sunday. Kaz and Tony are leaving late on Sunday afternoon, so we'd certainly have time to meet and maybe have lunch together. I could pick you up at the airport and we could go to one of the hotels nearby.

– That sounds fine. I'm sorry to mess you around so much.

– Don't worry about it. Now what time does your flight from Brussels get in?

UNIT 20 Meeting procedures

1 Overview

a   A: OK, um, as we're all here now – let's start. Did everyone receive the agenda?

B: Yes.

C: Yup.

D: Yes thanks.

A: Right, there are four topics on the agenda. But the main aim of today's meeting is to approve the plans for the new company gym. So, let's start with that. Has everyone seen the proposals?

B: No, I'm sorry I haven't.

A: Do we have any spare copies? Er … could you share with Carmen? So John, could you summarise the plans.

J: Yes of course. Everyone has seen …

b   – Right, can we deal with item 4 next – our spending on PR?

– Before we do, can I ask what we're doing in response to yesterday's article in *The Tribune*? Is anyone planning to reply to the paper?

– The board has decided that the best policy is to ignore the article.

– But have you read it? It's highly critical of our company. In the first paragraph it says that several of our products should be banned. It refers to a confidential internal report. We need to issue some kind of statement.

– Look, I think we are getting away from the point.

– No we are not. This company depends on its reputation. That's why we employ a PR company. Maybe if we paid them more, we'd get a better service from them.

c   – So, Carmen, did you want to say something about this smoking issue?

– Yes, thank you. I'm afraid I completely disagree with Carlo. As you know, I'm not a smoker, and I'm in favour of the smoking ban. Many smokers also support the policy of a total ban.

– Oh … with respect, that is not true. What evidence do you have that smokers support it?

– The union's internal survey. It showed that 67% of smokers would support a ban.

d   – Thanks for bringing that to my attention. That's a good point, but can we deal with it at the next meeting? It's getting late and we need to take a vote.

– I agree.

– Right, if there is nothing else anyone wants to add, let's vote on the proposals. All those in favour, please raise your hands. And all those against … So the motion is rejected by five votes to three. OK, let's call it a day. Thank you all for coming.

4 Listening

a   A: Good morning everybody. Sorry I'm so late; the traffic was terrible. Have you already introduced yourselves?

B: Yes, we have.

C: Yes.

A: OK. Shall we begin? There's a lot to get through and we only have one hour.

b   A: So who's going to take the minutes? Bill?

B: OK, I don't mind doing it.

A: Thanks. Right, has everyone got an agenda? Our main aim is to approve increases in the building budget. Let's start with item 1. Janet, I believe you wanted to say something about this.

C: Thanks, Maxine. As you know, I used to work for Wilmex and from my experience …

c – Mark, what's your opinion on all this? Do you have anything to add?
   – Yes, I do. I have to say that I'm opposed to spending any more money on the building programme than we've already agreed. In my opinion, the contractors are taking us for a ride.
   – Um, that's … that's very true. I agree.
d – Shall we vote on the proposal then? Those in favour? Those against? Are you abstaining, Janet?
   – Yes, I am.
   – OK, the proposal is accepted, four to two, with one abstention. If no one has anything else for us to discuss, I suggest we leave it there. It would be good to get home early for once!

UNIT 21 Meeting follow-up

1 Overview

a – How did the meeting go?
   – Not so well. We didn't have time to get through all the points – even though we overran by an hour. We've agreed to meet again early next week.
   – Did you start on time?
   – No, that was part of the problem. Several people arrived late. They went to the wrong room. Reception didn't know where we were. It was all very disorganised.
   – It sounds like it. Did Sam chair the meeting?
   – No. He's in Cape Town, so Anita stood in for him.
b – Were you at the meeting?
   – Yes, we missed you.
   – I'm sorry I couldn't make it. I had to do something for Marcus. How was it?
   – I thought it went well.
   – That's good. Who took the minutes?
   – Gus did. Unfortunately Katrin was away.
   – Oh. I hope he sends them out more quickly than he did last time. By the way, what was decided about the security problem on the Tafari site?
   – Pilar suggested putting the job out to tender. Vic asked her to look into the idea, and report back at the next meeting.
c – What's the position with Veltex?
   – I've fixed another meeting for next week.
   – Were you able to make the modifications they suggested?
   – No, not yet. I'm hoping to do that tomorrow.
   – But I thought you were going to send me your proposals first.
   – Yes, I know, I'm sorry. I've been so busy I haven't had time.
   – OK, but I'd still like to see them before they are finalised.
   – Yes, of course.
d – How are you getting on with the revised schedule?
   – It's all taken care of. I managed to send it out last week, as agreed.
   – What was the response?
   – Mr Awai called on Monday. He said that his initial reaction was favourable. And he promised to get back to us before the 24th. But he did say that they weren't prepared to pay any more.

3 Listening

1 – Hello.
   – Fabio, hi! Pilar here. Did you get my email?
   – Which email?
   – The one I sent you last week after the meeting on delivery procedures. It's just that I'm meeting the contractor's MD tomorrow and I haven't heard from you. I thought you were going to send me some ideas on how to handle the money question with him.
   – I'm sorry, Pilar. I didn't manage to do it. I've been so busy this week that I haven't had time to do anything other than keep my head above water. But I don't think you'll have any problems. I'm sure that if we offer to pay a token amount for implementing the changes they'll accept it.
   – I'm not so sure. They're also very busy at the moment, and to be honest, we're not their favourite client. I've heard that they're not happy about the fact that we've taken so long to make up our minds about what we want. Anyway, you did remember to send them a more detailed outline of our proposals, didn't you?
   – Actually, Pilar, I'm not sure I did. Is that what you asked me to do?
   – Yes, I did. And a copy to Harry Gross. Look, can you send the outline to NAK immediately. It's going to be very embarrassing for me to meet their MD tomorrow if they haven't received it.
   – Yes, of course.
   – And could you get a copy to Harry as soon as possible. He can't check the insurance if he doesn't have the details.
   – I'm very sorry about this. To be honest, I can't actually find your email.
   – Look, I'll resend it. I must go now. There's someone waiting for me on the other line. Let me call you back later this afternoon.

UNIT 22 Arranging a visit

1 Overview

a – [Voicemail] Hello, this is Faridah Khan. I'm calling on behalf of Dr Salem of the Nova Research Institute. Dr Salem will be visiting the States in July, and she would very much like to see Mr Aubrey while she's there, if it can be arranged. She'll be staying in Boston for six days from the 8th to the 13th. She is particularly hoping to visit your new laboratory in Vermont during her stay. Could you call me back? My number is 0659 688661.
b – What are the arrangements for the 24th?
   – You have a meeting with KMD at 10.30, and you're visiting Sin Go Wan.
   – Do you have a time for that yet?
   – Not yet.
   – And how am I getting to Ipoh on the 25th?
   – By car; someone will take you.
   – OK, and do you have the details of the meeting on the 26th?
   – Yes. You're meeting Greg Rice of Mantic Trading at 5.30.
   – Where is the meeting, do you know?
   – Probably in his office … we're not sure yet.
   – Oh, one last thing … what time does my flight arrive on the 23rd?
   – At 14.30.
c – Can I just check some of the details of your itinerary? Have you got a moment?
   – Yes, go ahead.
   – So, when do you get to Kuala Lumpur?
   – On the 23rd.
   – And do you know when your flight gets in?
   – At 14.30.
   – Do you know the flight number?
   – Yes, it's LF 234.

- Then you're flying to Singapore on the 27th. What time are you leaving and how long will you be staying there?
- I'm leaving at 11.30 in the morning and will probably be staying for three days. I need to check with the people in KL.

d – Can you tell me how to get to the hotel from the airport?
- Will you be coming by cab?
- No, I'm planning to hire a car.
- OK, you need to take the Fenner Tunnel out of the airport, and then get on the City Expressway, going south. After about four miles you take exit 3 – follow the signs for Corren. It's a straight road, and you turn left at the fourth set of lights – you'll see a department store just before the lights. That's Winchester Avenue. Go down Winchester to Stanford – it's about three blocks. Turn onto Stanford, and we're on the left. It's number 72. Would you like me to send you a copy of the directions?
- Yes, I'd appreciate that.
- You're welcome. I look forward to meeting you.

5 Application

1 – Hello. Is that Dr Rita Braun's secretary?
- Speaking.
- Oh, hello. This is Cindy Crayford from the Farrington Inn, Boston. Can I give you some directions to the Farrington Inn for Dr Braun?
- Yes, thank you. I'll make sure she gets them.
- Thank you. Are you familiar with Boston, by the way?
- No, I'm not, but Dr Braun has been there a couple of times.
- Good. We're looking forward to welcoming her here. Now, let me give you these details. I believe she'll be coming by taxi.
- That's right.
- OK. She needs to tell the cab driver to take the Sumner Tunnel, and then get to the Expressway South, which takes her to the Massachusetts Turnpike. Take the Mass Pike west to the first exit, Allston-Cambridge. Then follow the signs to Allston. At the fourth set of lights, turn left. This is Harvard Avenue – there's an antique store on the corner. After you turn onto Harvard, go down, and take the first left again, Farrington Avenue. We're on Farrington, the fifth house on the right, it's number 23.
- Thanks. I'll make sure Dr Braun gets these instructions.

UNIT 23 Abroad on business

1 Overview

a – Can I have a return to Amsterdam, please?
- Are you travelling before 9.30?
- Yes, I'm catching the 8.42 train.
- And when are you returning?
- On Friday afternoon.
- OK, that will be 155 euros.
- Am I entitled to any special discounts?
- No. I'm afraid they're only available on off-peak travel.
b – So how much do I owe you?
- With the map, 55 euros altogether. Are you driving north?
- Yes, we're heading for Lille.
- I hope you're not in a hurry. There are some road works further up the road.
- I hope there aren't any serious delays. We have to be there by 6 o'clock.

- There have been terrible jams all week, so, good luck!
c – Do your hire rates include insurance?
- Yes. They include everything except fuel.
- OK, can you send the bill to Press Ltd for the attention of Heidi Floss?
- Are you an account customer?
- Yes, we are.
- Do you know your account number?
- No I'm sorry, I don't.
- That's OK. It'll be on the computer. Could you sign here, please?
d – I never have a problem with jet lag. I just sleep on the flight and I'm fine later.
- You're lucky. I find it very hard to sleep on long-haul flights.
- No, I just take a sleeping pill. I'll take one as soon as we're on the plane.
- And, I won't sleep till I get there. I'll try to go to bed for a while when I get to the hotel.

Note The French speaker in **b** does not pronounce the final *s* in *euros*.

4 Application

a – Have you got a single room for Thursday night?
- Just a moment, please … Yes, we have. Would you like a smoking or a non-smoking room?
- Non-smoking, please. And do you have any rooms with baths?
- No, I'm afraid our rooms only have showers.
- That's a shame. Anyway, how much is the room per night?
- It's 150 dollars. That includes a hot buffet breakfast.
- OK. I'd like to book a room. The name is Vanta – that's V-A-N-T-A, Mr. Can you send the bill to Rembola Ltd, for the attention of Digby Linna?
b – Can I have a return ticket to Paris, please?
- First or second class?
- First class, please. Do I need to reserve a seat?
- When are you planning to travel?
- On the 16.56.
- Yes, then it would be a good idea to reserve a seat. It's normally very busy.
- I'd like to pay by credit card?
c – How long do you want the car for?
- Five days.
- What size car are you looking for?
- Um, … four-door saloon. Something economical, but not too small.
- The Mazda in group D might suit you.
- How much is it?
- It's 80 pounds per day. That includes everything except fuel.
- That sounds fine.

UNIT 24 Returning from a business trip

1 Overview

a – You're looking well. Have you been away?
- I'm just back from a trip to São Paulo in Brazil.
- Ah, what were you doing there?
- I was visiting some customers. Have you been to Brazil?
- No. What was it like?
- Very interesting. I didn't realise it was such a huge place. It's divided into nine economic areas, and the biggest, São Paulo, is about the same size as Finland. Sao Paulo alone accounts for 55% of Brazil's industrial output.

And if it was an independent country, it would be among the 20 richest countries worldwide.
- So, how long were you there?
- Just a week; it wasn't long enough.

b
- Where did you stay?
- In a hotel called the Fort Aguarda, not far from Deelong. It's a first class hotel and it was very convenient for us – most of our work was close to Deelong. Do you know that area?
- No, I've never been there.
- It's very beautiful. The views from the hotel were fantastic. The hotel itself was great – excellent food, beautiful rooms, friendly service and reasonable prices.
- Where is it exactly?
- It's on the coast, about eight kilometres south-east of Deelong.
- How did you get there?
- There are regular local flights to Ikajar, which isn't far from Deelong. It's easiest to take a taxi from the airport.

c
- I'd better write my travel report today in case they need it tomorrow. If I finish it before you go home, I'll let you have a copy.
- I'd be very interested to read it.
- Thanks, and it would be good to have some comments from you if possible before I do the final draft.
- No problem. Was it a good trip by the way?
- Yes, it was hard work, but it was very worthwhile. I made some good contacts while I was there.

4 Listening

- Bill, hi! Good to see you back in Berlin. I hear you've just got back from Russia.
- That's right. have you heard that we've got a project going on in a place called Nevtchugansk at the moment? Do you know it?
- No, but I guess it must be an oil town with a name like that.
- That's right. Anyway, it was a good trip. It didn't take as long as I'd expected. We had to transfer to Vnukova airport in Moscow, but then it was only a very pleasant three-hour flight.
- How long were you there?
- Just over three days. But I expect I'll be going back quite a lot in the future; there's a lot of work to do.
- Where exactly is it?
- Do you know Siberia?
- A bit. I spent a week in Chelyabinsk three years ago.
- OK. Nevtchugansk is north-east of Chelyabinsk, not far from Sergut. It's this side of the Urals. The town itself is OK. I think about 100,000 people live there. Most of them seem to be connected with the oil industry in some way or other. I'm looking forward to going back. The people are very friendly, and the work is fascinating.
- What was the weather like?
- They're having a late summer; I took my cold weather gear in case it snowed, but I didn't need it.

Note
nevt = oil in Russian

UNIT 25 Personal finances

1 Overview

a
- About 24% of my income goes in tax, which is quite low. I don't know how people manage in places where tax rates are higher. I have a good job – I suppose I earn about 50,000 with bonuses, but I wouldn't say that we

were well-off. We can't afford to run two cars. The cost of living is very high here. I always seem to have an overdraft.
- So where does your money go?
- We do spend a lot on food, but then we're a large family – it's difficult to economise. We spend very little on holidays, we usually go camping. We did go abroad for a week last year, but that was exceptional. I don't know where the money goes. We don't often go out.
- What about your spare time?
- I'm keen on sailing, which I suppose is quite an expensive hobby! But on the whole we're careful with money; we have to be.

b
- Our apartment was broken into yesterday. They took the TV and my notebook computer. They were both brand new.
- Oh no! What were they worth?
- About 1,500 euros.
- I hope you're insured.
- Yes, luckily I paid the premium last week and I'm going to make a claim.
- Are you covered for electrical goods?
- I assume so. I'll check with the insurance company. I have to call them to get a claim form.

c
- Art's outgoings are very similar to mine. We both have a family to support and a mortgage to pay. My guess is that his income is about the same as mine. I don't understand how he can afford such an expensive car.
- He probably borrowed the money. Your basic situation may be similar to his, but he's very different to you. He never saves anything. You never spend anything!

d
- What's the figure of 2612 for?
- Er … where's that?
- Um, six lines down.
- Oh, that's for travel costs.
- And what does this figure represent?
- It's for accountancy costs.
- Mmm. They're both up a lot.
- Yes, but expenditure on telephone and postage is down. It's half what it was last year.

3 Listening

- You asked me where all the money goes. It's difficult to say exactly, but obviously we spend a lot of money on food, groceries. I enjoy cooking, and as we have a large family – four children – our food bill is quite big. We also like eating out; we probably go out to a restaurant about once a week, often with friends. Unfortunately, there are no theatres around here, so we don't go to the theatre as much as we'd like. But we do spend money on our hobbies. I'm very keen on skiing – that's an expensive hobby. I'm also very interested in antiques – especially clocks and watches. You must let me show you my collection one day …
- I'd like that. What about holidays? Do you usually go abroad or stay in this country?
- Oh, we usually stay here. In fact, we spend very little on holidays. We have a small house in the country and we usually go there. That's where I can really relax. We did go Canada last year, but that was exceptional.

UNIT 26 Company finances

1 Overview

a
- What was your turnover last year?
- It was 17.5 million – a good year for us. Overall, revenue increased by 5.7% over the period.
- Wow! How was that achieved?

- There were two key factors: we spent more on advertising, which resulted in increased business; and we improved the quality of our customer care.
- How much profit did you make?
- Our profit was a little disappointing. The new strategy means that our operating costs are higher. For example, we're offering more choice, so more money is tied up in stock, which means our interest charges are higher.

b
- Domestic sales accounted for only 33% of our total revenue last year, and the figure will be even lower this year.
- Are you having problems in the domestic market?
- Well, competition here is very tough. There's a lot of pressure on margins. So, we're putting more resources into our export markets, where margins are better. We have also increased manufacturing productivity by 6.5%.
- What are your total sales so far this year?
- Er … in the period from January to the end of September, they're in the region of 64 million.
- That's very good.
- Yes, but profits are down. The fact is, we won't see the benefits of the reorganisation till next year's accounts. We've set tough targets for the coming year.

c
- So what's the total value of the company now?
- Well, the net asset value is 12.5 million dollars. But we believe the market value is between 15 and 20 million.
- And what's the value of your fixed assets?
- The book value is 11 million.
- What about your debtors?
- They're just over 7 million.
- And your creditors, tax liabilities? How much do you owe?
- Currently about 5.5 million.

d
You all have copies of the accounts in the folders in front of you. I believe the balance sheet presents a very favourable picture of the company. I'd just like to bring a couple of points to your attention. As a result of a rise in sales in the final quarter of the year, we were able to increase our net profit, and I am now in a position to recommend a final dividend of 10.5 cents per share. I'm sure you will agree that there has been a great improvement in the last 12 months. A key factor in these results is the quality of our management team. Today this company is valued at between 30 and 35 million dollars. Our aim is to continue to expand the company by meeting our customers' needs profitably without …

4 Listening

In November, the Aviation Authority announced its new pricing formula for airport charges over the next five years. In the period under review, income from this source accounted for 33% of our total revenue.

By setting price increases at well below the retail price index, the new formula provides us with tough targets over the coming period. To maintain current levels of profit, we have to improve cost efficiency and productivity significantly.

I am confident that we can meet these challenges. In the last year of account, productivity measured in passengers-per- airport-employee increased by 6.5%, while actual staff numbers fell from 10,733 to 8,730.

This was achieved while at the same time improving the quality of our service; a fact confirmed by our customer surveys, which involved interviews with more than 125,000 passengers.

Our overall revenue has increased. A key factor in this area is the expansion of airport retailing. Our aim is to meet customers' needs profitably – principally, by more choice and competition, with better service and value for money.

As this strategy was applied to shops, catering revenue per passenger increased by 5.7% year-on-year. Retail expansion will continue this year, with the opening of 90 new shops. A second key factor in these results is the quality of our management team …

UNIT 27 Payment issues

1 Overview

a
- Good morning. It's Maeve Russell here from MSG. I'm calling about an invoice we sent you on May the 27th.
- Can you give me the details, please?
- Yes. The invoice number is PS-471. It was due for payment on the 25th of June. I've sent you a couple of emails about it.
- Let me just check. Yes, according to our records this was paid on the 19th.
- Well I checked this morning and we haven't received anything.
- That's strange. My records show that it was passed for payment on the 12th, and paid the following week.
- Well something seems to have gone wrong. Could you look into it and get back to me?
- Yes, of course. Leave it with me.

b
- Could you tell me what the invoice was for?
- Yes, it was for 500 guide books at 15 dollars each.
- And what was the payment date?
- The 17th of March.
- Ah yes, here it is. Apparently, we haven't settled it as we haven't received the books yet.
- But according to the delivery note, the goods were delivered to your warehouse on March 12th.
- Do you have the note in front of you?
- Yes; it's signed by T. Beeson.
- I'm sorry about this. There seems to be some kind of mix-up. Let me look into it and I'll get back to you.

c
- Our invoice 0173-K is still outstanding. Is there a problem with it?
- No, it seems to be OK. I'll make sure that it's included in the next computer run.
- So, when can we expect to receive the money?
- We have a computer run every Friday. Is that OK?
- Yes, that would be fine.
- If you want payment sooner that that, I'll arrange for a transfer to be made immediately.
- No, I'll assume everything is OK unless I hear from you.

d
- We wrote to you on the 12th. Apparently the invoice details didn't tie up with our order. That's why we haven't paid yet.
- But we talked about this last week. You said it was all OK now. Could you please sort it out by tomorrow?
- I'm very sorry about this. I'll do it this afternoon.

4 Listening

An Austrian financial controller working in Amsterdam
What is not happening is that the invoices are not being sent to my name personally, but to the company's name. Now, I have stressed this on several occasions. It's a large company. We receive hundreds of invoices every week, and by the time the registry of the internal post office finds

the recipient of the invoice, as much as two weeks can elapse before we can take action, so please, in the future, address the invoices to my attention – to my name.

A New Zealand director of a small real estate company
I think if you're talking about the November account, you will find that we have actually paid that. The cheque was sent to you on the 20th of this month and you should find that within – in your records. We have a policy of always paying our accounts on the 20th of the following month, and, at the moment, we have no problem doing that.

An English production manager for a publishing firm
Oh, I do apologise about that. I have seen your invoice and I have passed it to the accounts department. I can only imagine that it's either got lost be- … in the post between myself and the accounts department, or they just haven't got round to paying for it yet. But I will actually look into it and let you know.

A Scottish accountant
I'm afraid that the person who authorises the invoices is away on tour at the moment. He won't be back for a week yet. But I'm sure it will go through quickly after he's back.

An Irish export manager
Well, actually we've been looking into this invoice and it seems to be under query. Erm, it appears that you actually charged us incorrectly. Erm, we did agree a rate, erm which you actually faxed to me and signed on the 22nd, and it appears that you've completely disregarded that and sent us a com- … a different invoice with a totally different rate. Erm, so we're actually waiting for a credit to come through before we will agree to process it.

5 Application

- Festro Management Systems. Can I help you?
- Yes, I hope so. This is Taina Pura of VX Training Manuals. I'm calling about an invoice that we sent you six weeks ago, which is due for payment. I notice that it's still outstanding. It was due for payment on the 15th. The invoice number is 90/0976. Could you tell me what's happened to it?
- Could you hold on a moment? I'll just check … I'm sorry, but I have no record of the invoice. Could you give me some details?
- Yes, it was for 50 copies of our VX training manual at 50 euros each, and 25 copies of the AK booklet at 8 euros a copy. The invoice value was 2,700 euros.
- When was the payment due?
- July 15th. We sent you the invoice on June 15th.
- Was there any other information?
- Only the discount – it was 5% if the invoice was settled within 14 days, but obviously that doesn't apply …
- No, of course not. Well, I'm very sorry about this. We always try to be very prompt with our payments. I'll try and locate the invoice, and arrange for payment to be sent immediately. Leave it with me. If I can't find the paperwork, I'll get back to you.
- Thanks.

UNIT 28 Preparing for a presentation

1 Overview

a – Hi, Sergei. I'm calling to check what equipment you need for your talk.
  – Oh, hi. I was going to call you to ask if you have a whiteboard copier.

- Yes, we do. I'll find out if it's available. Do you mind using an ordinary whiteboard if it isn't?
- No, that's OK. I'm used to making changes to the workshop, depending on the equipment that's available. But I'll definitely need a flipchart and a beamer.
- Right … Are you planning to use your own laptop?
- Yes, I am.
- Fine. Is there anything else you need?
- No, I think that's it.
- Well, I look forward to meeting you next week, and if you think of anything else just give me a ring. I'll get back to you about the whiteboard.

b – Have you got everything you need?
  – I think so … but how does the projector work? I can't turn it on. I found the on/off switch, but it isn't working. I think the bulb needs changing.
  – OK, I'll see if I can find another projector.
  – Thanks. And could you get hold of an extension lead? There's no socket over here.
  – Sure. Is there anything else you need?
  – Yes, some marker pens. These have run out. Thanks.
  – OK, I'll get some right away.

c – Margo's not keen on giving presentations, but she's very good at working with small groups.
  – She can't stand in front of an audience, that's the problem. She gets nervous.
  – I suppose she'll just have to get used to it.

d – We'll begin in about five minutes' time if you are ready. I think everyone is here now.
  – Right.
  – Have you got everything you need? Would you like some water?
  – No thanks.
  – Shall I introduce you?
  – If you like. I don't mind.
  – OK, I'll just say a few words.

4 Listening

- Is that Mr Roussos?
- Speaking.
- Hello, Mr Roussos. It's David Harram here. I'm calling to check what equipment you need for your presentation next week.
- Thank you. I'm glad you called – I was just about to send you an email. Right, I need a flipchart and a DVD player if possible.
- Do you mind using an old video player? Unfortunately, our DVD player is broken.
- Don't worry, I have the material on video as well as DVD. Do you also have a beamer and a screen?
- Yes, we do.
- Excellent! I'll bring my own camera and tripod. Actually, I don't think I'll need anything else. If I think of anything, I'll give you a ring. So, I look forward to meeting you next week.
- And we're looking forward to meeting you. I hope you'll have time to stay for lunch after the morning session.
- Thanks. I'd like that very much indeed.

UNIT 29 Presenting facts and figures

1 Overview

a – The graph shows the total number of unemployed workers in the region. The vertical axis shows the rate of unemployment. The year is shown on the horizontal

axis. As you can see from the blue line here, the overall rate of unemployment was just under 9% in 2005.
At this point on the curve, there's a sharp fall, indicating that the situation improved significantly.

- – Was the improvement the same for skilled and unskilled workers?
- – No, the dotted line here represents skilled workers, and you can see that the level of unemployment in this group fell faster than average.
b – This table shows retail sales. The figures in the left-hand column are average sales per branch.
- – Excuse me, what does RTF stand for?
- – Where is that?
- – In the top left-hand corner, just below the pie chart.
- – I'm sorry, it's not very clear. It actually says RST, which stands for Retail Sales Totals. The pie chart shows total retail sales broken down into product areas.
For example, the blue segment in the chart represents childrenswear. The bullet points on the right-hand side, here, show what the colours in the chart represent.
c – Sales average 517 euros per square metre. At peak times, like Christmas, the figure is higher, but on average we make a sale every 3.5 seconds – the average value of each sale being 20 euros.
- – Could you say something about the trends? How do these facts and figures compare with last year, or the year before?
- – Well, we are selling twice as much as we did two years ago, in terms of volume.
d – It says in this article that the number of stores has gone down slightly. Apparently, it's now 283.
- – Hm … that's surprising.
- – And the figure for customers per day is about the same.
- – What's the up-to-date figure for sandwiches sold per day?
- – It's, ah, 6,500.
- – Does the article say anything about sales of salmon sandwiches?
- – Yeah, it's in the last paragraph. Sales have risen slightly.

3 Listening

… to me that in comparison, it might be interesting to consider some historical data of unemployment in the UK between 1975 and 1992 …

Now as you can see, in 1990, just over 12% of unskilled manual workers were unemployed, but by 1991, this was over 16%. A similar rise took place among employers and managers: their employment level rose from just over 2% to nearly 6% in the same period. The trend among professionals was the same, although slightly less dramatic: unemployment in this group rose from just over 1% to 3%.

In more prosperous times, the middle classes do much better in the job market. Unemployment among employers and managers is always well below 5%, compared with semi-skilled and unskilled workers, where an average of more than 10% are unemployed, even in boom years.

It is significant, therefore, that in 1991, the rate of unemployment among employers and managers was nearly 6%, while among junior non-manual staff it rose to over 7%. Both groups tend to be middle class – notice that throughout the period shown in the table, the trend among junior non-manual staff remained just above the level for employers and managers.

Semi-skilled and unskilled workers, on the other hand, seem to suffer badly in boom years. The figure for semi-skilled workers peaked at around 16% in 1983; the peak for unskilled workers was even higher – approximately 17% in 1985.

Now if I can compare these figures with some more recent statistics, …

UNIT 30 Delivering a presentation

1 Overview

a Good morning, everyone. Welcome. I've divided my talk into three parts. First of all, I'd like to give a brief overview of the company's current activities. Then I'll say a few words about the takeover. Then finally, I'll talk a little about future prospects. We'll be breaking for coffee at about 11.15. So, let's start with the company's main activities. As this table shows, about 75% of turnover comes from products manufactured by our parent company, QET. We are a sales organisation, and our main activity is to sell QET products. We do this by supplying retail outlets and also through our mail order operation. If you look at the figures in this table …
b That's a very interesting question and I'd like to come back to it during the next session, if I may. Right now, I'd like to finish describing the history of the company. In 1999, Sir Henry Wraxall became head of Bexted Electronics. And the following year, Lord Hamrid was appointed to the board. Mazar Akstrom also joined the company in that year. For those of you who are not familiar with the system of U.K. titles I'd like to explain …
c – As we are running late, I'm afraid there is no time for any more questions. But I'll be here during the coffee break, so anyone with specific enquiries can speak to me then. But now, I'll hand over to Sam Corfu. Sam would like to say something about our product range.
- – Thank you. As Monica mentioned earlier, we constantly review and update our range of products. We've been selling some of our lines for more than ten years, but fashions change and catalogue selling depends on being up to date.
d – How did the presentation go?
- – I thought it went quite well in spite of the fact that some of the audience looked rather tired.
- – Ah, yes, I suppose just after lunch is a difficult time.
- – Also, it was a very big room. Some people couldn't hear very well.
- – How many people were there?
- – About 70. The actual attendance was quite good and there was some good feedback. But next time I'll arrange to speak before lunch, not after it, if possible!

4 Listening

Speaker 1
First, I'll give you a brief overview of the company and then I'll say a few words about the takeover rumours.

Oknover's main activity is selling doors and windows, and door and window frames produced by Fortishka in Russia. We do not act as an agent for, or sell articles for, any other company. We don't sell bells and knockers. We don't sell any other fixtures or fittings. We only sell wooden doors and window frames. This table shows our projected sales for the coming year in US dollars. Our projected sales are 2,275,000 dollars. Last year, the result was just over 2 million dollars. So this year, we are looking at a growth of a little over 10% which, in view of the economic climate is quite considerable. Any questions so far?

Speaker 2
Oknover operates as a sales and marketing operation for Fortishka in the UK and Irish markets, from Liverpool, England.

With regard to staffing levels, they have seven full-time staff, consisting of the managing director, his secretary and personal assistant, two sales managers and two sales coordinators, who are based in the office. A bookkeeper/accountant completes the team.

The company aims to develop profitable business for Fortishka products – that is, doors and windows, and door and window frames. As you can see, there is very little diversification, but I'll say more about their product range in a moment.

The company does not act as agents for any other company apart from Fortishka.

As you can see from this table, the projected sales budget for this year is 2,275,000 dollars, of which doors account for 1,550,000 dollars and window frames account for 725,000 dollars. These figures are taken from their annual report.

That brings me to my next point, which is that all our information comes from public sources. At the moment, we do not have any inside information. Therefore, the picture we have may not be completely up-to-date.

Grammar/language index

Glossary of business-related terms

acquisition: acquiring something; in business this is usually another company, e.g. *XYZ plc is our latest acquisition*

ad hoc: an ad hoc meeting is a meeting arranged informally to suit the participants

AGM: annual general meeting

Annual Percentage Rate (APR): rate of interest (such as on hire-purchase agreements) shown on an annual compound basis, including fees and charges

annual report: report of a company's financial situation at the end of each year, sent to all shareholders

anti-trust: attacks monopolies and encourages competition

AOB: Any Other Business (on an agenda)

APR: annual percentage rate (see above)

Arabic numerals: numbers written as 1, 2, 3, 4, etc. (see also Roman numerals)

assets: things which belong to a company or person, and which have a realistic value

asset value: value of a company calculated by adding together all its assets (see also current assets and fixed assets)

audit: examination of the books and accounts of a company

authorisation: give formal approval; sanction something

back-up: support

balance: amount to be put in one of the columns of an account to make the total debits and credits equal

balance brought forward/carried forward: amount entered in an account at the end of a period or page of an account book to balance the debit and credit entries; it is then taken forward to start the new period or page

balance sheet: statement of the financial position of a company at a particular time

beamer: a digital projector

bid: offering an amount of money for something in competition with other people/organisations; the highest bidder is successful in securing the goods or services

(the) book (financial jargon): the value of an asset according to the company's books/accounts

bought ledger: set of accounts recording money owed to each supplier, i.e. the creditors of the company

branch: local office or shop belonging to a larger organisation

brand: the make/name of a product

broker: dealer who acts as a middleman between a buyer and a seller (stock broker: person who buys or sells shares for clients; insurance broker: person who sells insurance to clients)

budget: plan of expected spending and income (usually for one year)

bullet points: a list of points identified by dots or asterisks

buyout (management buyout): takeover of a company by a group of employees (usually managers and directors)

capital: the money put into a business

capital goods: goods used to manufacture other goods, i.e. machinery

carry forward: to take an account balance at the end of the current period as the starting point for the next period (see also balance)

catalogue selling: selling from a book where items for sale are listed

catering: providing food and drink for a number of people

CBI: Confederation of British Industries

CEO: chief executive officer

chartered accountant: accountant who has passed professional examinations and is a member of the Institute of Chartered Accountants

childrenswear: retail term for children's clothing

commission: financial proportion of a sale paid to the person who makes the sale, e.g. 5% of total value of sales

company secretary: role of administrative responsibility within an organisation

conglomerate: group of subsidiary companies linked together and forming a group, each making very different types of products

contract out: the company gives a proportion of its work to an outside organisation or person; this may be because the work contracted out requires skills not provided by the company, or because the company is too busy

conveyancing: legally transferring a property from a seller to a buyer

core business: main business

credit control: check that customers pay on time and do not owe more than their credit limit

credit limit: fixed amount which is the most a customer can owe in credit

creditor: organisation/business/person owed money

current assets: assets used by a company in its ordinary work (such as materials, finished products, cash, monies due) and which are held for a short time only

customise: change to fit the special needs of a customer

cut down on: reduce

CV: curriculum vitae; a summary of a person's work experience and education/qualifications

defer (deferred taxation): to put back to a later date or to postpone

depreciation: reduction in value of an asset

diversification: taking on forms of work that are different, but related to, the core business of the organisation/company

dividend: percentage of profits paid to shareholders

equity: value of a company's shares

estimate: an approximation rather than something precise or specific

ETA: estimated time of arrival

expenditure: the total financial outgoings (spending) of a company/business

expressway/turnpike (UK English motorway): a stretch of road with three or more lanes of traffic going in the same direction; there may be a payment for travelling on these roads

factoring: business of buying debt at a discount (a 'factor' collects a company's debts when due, and pays the creditor in advance part of the sum to be collected, so 'buying' the debt)

(to) fire: to tell someone that you no longer need him/her to work for the company, e.g. *We had to fire him because he just wasn't meeting our requirements*

fire retardant: chemical which slows down the burning process

fiscal: referring to tax or to government revenues

fiscal year: 12-month period on which taxes are calculated, e.g. in the UK 6 April to the following 5 April

fixed assets: property or machinery which a company owns and uses, but which the company does not buy and sell as part of its regular trade, including the company's investments in shares or other companies

flagship: something of importance, e.g. *The paper-shredder is our flagship product*

flipchart: a board with paper attached

franchise: licence to trade using a brand name and paying a royalty for it

franchising: act of selling a licence to trade as a franchise

freehold site: site which the owner holds forever and on which no rent is paid

freelance: an independent worker who works for several different companies

fringe benefits: extra items given by a company to workers in addition to a salary, e.g. company cars, private health insurance

GDP: gross domestic product

GNP: gross national product

goodwill: adding value beyond money alone, e.g. *The company has built up goodwill because of the fair way it treats its customers*

gross profit: profit before deductions (e.g. tax)

hacking: getting into someone else's computer system without their permission

hand over to: give time/responsibility to someone else

hard disk: computer disk which has a sealed case and can store large quantities of information

hardware: computer hardware; machines used in data processing including the computers and printer, but not the programs

hedge: protecting yourself against a loss (possibly financial), e.g. *a hedge against inflation*

human resources: the workers a company has available, seen from the point of view of their skills and experience

Inc. (US): incorporated

inflation: an increase in prices

institutional investors: institutions such as pension funds and insurance companies that buy large quantities of shares

intangible assets: the value of something that isn't physical, e.g. a trademark

interest: payment made by a borrower for the use of money, calculated as a percentage of the capital borrowed (high interest = interest at a high percentage)

interest rate: percentage charge for borrowing money

investment trust: company whose shares can be bought on the Stock Exchange, and whose business is to make money by buying and selling stocks and shares

joint venture: very large business project where two companies join together, often forming a new joint company to manage the project

laminating: sticking together thin layers of materials, e.g. wood, plastic

lease: an agreement (generally for a fixed period and a fixed amount of money) between someone who owns something and someone who wants to rent it

ledger: book in which accounts are written

liabilities: debts of a business

liaise: communicate about something; meet in a specific place

license: to give someone official permission to do something

licensee: person who has a licence, especially a licence to sell alcohol or to manufacture something

logistics: the practicalities of a chain of events, e.g. getting materials shipped from one country to another so they can be used in a factory to make finished goods, which are then forwarded to retail outlets

loss adjuster: person who calculates how much insurance should be paid on a claim

margin: difference between the money received when selling a product and the money paid for it

margins: profit margins

market: area where products might be sold, or group of people who might buy a product

market leader: company with the largest market share

market value: value of a product or company if sold today

materials handling: moving raw materials and semi-finished goods from one place to another

MD: managing director

merchant bank: bank which arranges loans to companies and deals in international finance, buys and sells shares, launches new companies on the Stock Exchange, but does not provide normal banking services to the general public

motion: a formal proposal put forward at a meeting

net: price, weight or pay, etc. after all deductions have been made

net profit: profit after deductions (e.g. tax)

network: system which links different points together

NIC: national insurance contributions

offering: a contribution

off-the-shelf: ready-made

operating cost: costs of the day-to-day organisation of a company

operating profit: profits made by a company in its usual business

O/S: outstanding; not yet paid or completed

outsource: to give work to another company/person outside the company

overdraft: when a person/organisation has spent more money than is in their bank account

PA: personal assistant

parent company: company which owns more than 50% of the shares of another company

partnership: unregistered business where two or more people (but not more than 20) share the risks and profits according to a partnership scheme

passive smoking: breathing in other people's cigarette/pipe/cigar smoke

perks: special benefits or advantages received

petty cash: a float of cash kept in an office to cover general and day-to-day expenses

PIN (personal identification number): unique number allocated to the holder of a cash or credit card, by which the holder can enter an automatic banking system

PLC (UK): public limited company

PR: public relations

pre-dyed: colour-dyed before

premises: a building for either staff or goods, e.g. *Our warehouse premises are where we keep the bulk of our goods*

president: head of a company; in the UK, president is sometimes a title given to a non-executive former chairman of a company; in the USA, the president is the main executive director of a company

products: range of products = different products from which a customer can choose; a line of products = different products that form a group (a range of products might include a number of different lines)

profit and loss account: statement of a company's expenditure and income over a period of time, almost always one calendar year, showing whether that company has made a profit or loss

proofs: test copies of written materials

proprietor: owner (see also sole trader)

protectionism: protecting producers in the home country against foreign competitors by banning or taxing imports or by imposing import quotas

prototype: the first model of a new machine, built for testing

proviso: a condition

publicly owned: the company's shares are owned by the public and can be traded on the Stock Exchange

quantity surveyor: person who carries out a quantity survey (to carry out a quantity survey = to estimate the amount of materials and the cost of the labour required for a construction project)

query: a doubt or uncertainty about something, e.g. *I have a query on this invoice; Can I query that date with you?*

ratify: to give formal consent or approval, e.g. *Management have ratified the new contracts for factory workers*

receipt: a document to prove purchase of goods or services, e.g. *Make sure you get a receipt when you pay the taxi fare*

recruitment: finding new people to join a company

redundancy: being no longer employed, because the job is no longer necessary

redundancy package: various benefits and payments given to a worker who is being made redundant

reimburse: to give money back for services and goods already paid for, e.g. *Will you reimburse me for the train fare?; These goods are faulty, so I'd like you to reimburse the total costs*

retail outlets: shops

retail sales: sales to the general public

revenue: income

Roman numerals: numbers written as i, ii, iii, iv, etc. (see also Arabic numerals)

RPI: retail price index = index which shows how prices of consumer goods have increased or decreased over a period of time

search engine: a computer program that locates information; Google and Yahoo! are Internet search engines

securities: investments in stocks and shares; certificates to show that someone owns stocks or shares

server: a computer program that links the user to data, e.g. a web server provides documents to your computer from the World Wide Web

settlement: an agreement, usually financial, e.g. *ABC Ltd made a huge out-of-court settlement*

sewage plant: a place where waste matter is treated

(on the) shop floor: in the factory, in the works or among the ordinary workers

Sir/Lord (UK): honorary titles

sole proprietor: person who owns a business on his own, with no partners, without forming a company

sole trader: person who runs a business by himself but has not registered it as a company

spreadsheet: a document on which financial information is kept, e.g. *Can we see the spreadsheet for last month's sales?*

staple: fasten with a short, thin piece of wire

statute: the law

stifle: to suppress or control something

stock: materials to be used in production or goods to be sold

stock market: stock exchange, a trading and dealing house

stocks and shares: shares in ordinary companies

(to) subcontract: to agree with an outside company that they will do part of the work for a project

subcontractor: company which has a contract to do work for a main contractor

subscription: a sum of money paid for membership of a club or for delivery of newspapers, journals, etc.

subsistence allowance: money provided by an employer which is designed to cover basic living costs and expenses

sundry expenses: various small expenses which are not itemised

systems analysis: using a computer to suggest how a company should work by analysing the way in which it works at present

systems analyst: persons who specialises in systems analysis

takeover: the purchase of a controlling interest in one company by another company

tally: correspond with, match, e.g. *We managed to get the final figures to tally*

tender (to put a job out to tender): to invite an outside company to bid for the work

'top-drawer': expression meaning 'first class'

trim: decorative detail

turnover: total amount of goods/services sold by a company

turnpike: see **expressway**

Twh: the terawatt hour, a unit for measuring energy; it corresponds to 1,000,000,000 kWh (kilowatt hours)

utility company: company that is regulated by its own country to provide a public service, e.g. the Swedish company Vattenfall provides energy in Europe under government control

value-added tax (US equivalent 'sales tax'): tax imposed as a percentage of the invoice value of goods and services

VAT: value-added tax

waiver: giving up (a right) or removing the conditions (of a rule)

waiver clause: clause in a contract giving the conditions under which the rights in the contract can be given up

weblink: a link that takes you from one part of the Internet to another

weighting (regional weighting allowance): additional salary or wages paid to compensate for living in an expensive part of the country

weld: to join two pieces of metal together by melting the parts which touch each other

works manager: person in charge of a works/plant

write off: to cancel an outstanding debt or to acknowledge a failure of some kind, e.g. *At the G8 summit, politicians met to discuss writing off third world debt; The last idea was a complete write off, so we're going to start again!*